FORD TOPLOADER TRANSMISSIONS

1964–1973

John Carollo

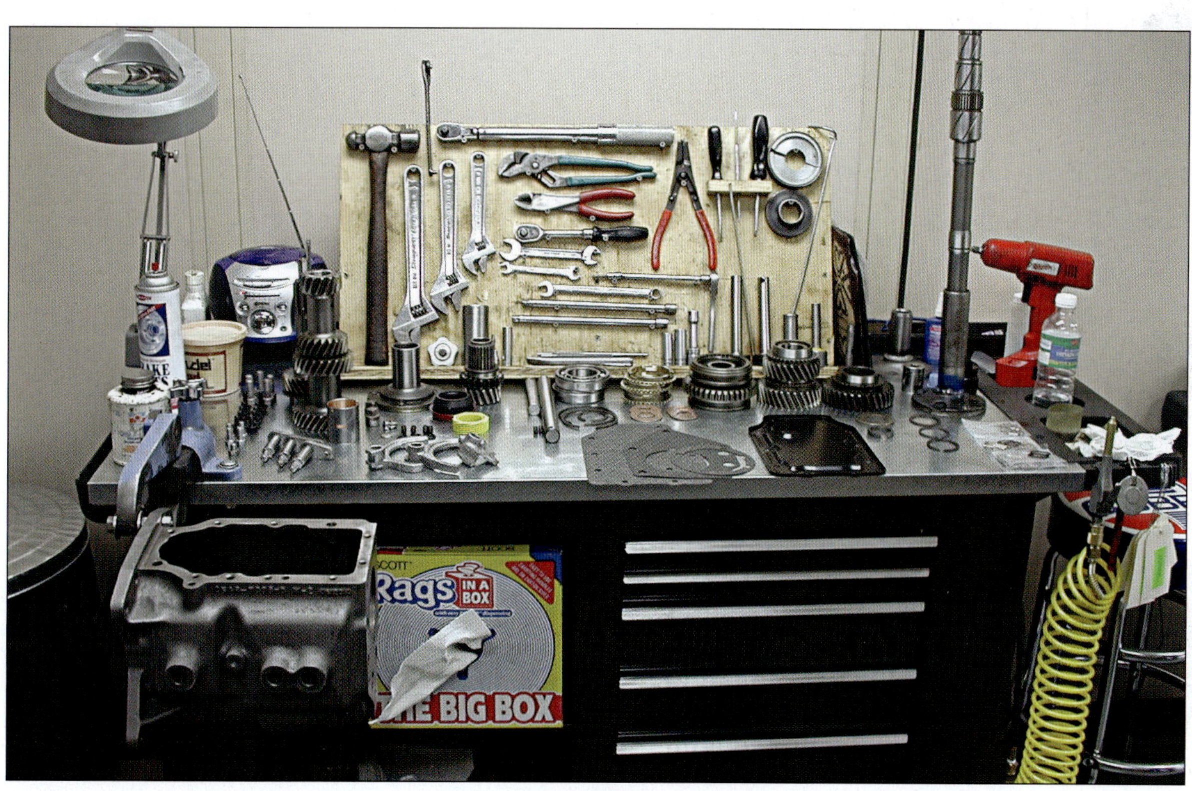

CarTech®

CarTech®

CarTech®, Inc.
6118 Main Street
North Branch, MN 55056
Phone: 651-277-1200 or 800-551-4754
Fax: 651-277-1203
www.cartechbooks.com

Edit by Wes Eisenschenk
Layout by Monica Seiberlich

ISBN 978-1-61325-756-2
Item No. SA534

Library of Congress Cataloging-in-Publication Data Available

Written, edited, and designed in the U.S.A.
Printed in China
10 9 8 7 6 5 4 3 2 1

CarTech books may be purchased at a discounted rate in bulk for resale, events, corporate gifts, or educational purposes. Special editions may also be created to specification. For details, contact Special Sales at 6118 Main Street, North Branch, MN 55056 or by email at sales@cartechbooks.com.

DISTRIBUTION BY:

Europe
PGUK
63 Hatton Garden
London EC1N 8LE, England
Phone: 020 7061 1980 • Fax: 020 7242 3725
www.pguk.co.uk

Australia
Renniks Publications Ltd.
3/37-39 Green Street
Banksmeadow, NSW 2109, Australia
Phone: 2 9695 7055 • Fax: 2 9695 7355
www.renniks.com

Canada
Login Canada
300 Saulteaux Crescent
Winnipeg, MB, R3J 3T2 Canada
Phone: 800 665 1148 • Fax: 800 665 0103
www.lb.ca

CONTENTS

ACKNOWLEDGMENTS

The creation of all books is a team effort, and this was no exception. It began with Wes Eisenschenk and his team at CarTech. They had the idea to publish a book about Ford Toploader transmissions, and they worked me into the mix. After I submitted the words, captions, and photos, Wes and his team created this nice, clean, and professional package. Throughout the extensive process of making this book, many other folks contributed their valuable knowledge and support.

One of my favorite sayings is, "Knowledge is not always about knowing—it is about knowing how to find out." That applies to this book because I needed Ford Toploader experts to help me confirm that all of the information is correct. Then, I compiled a group of specialists to consult if I ran into any problems.

I began with David Kee. His website, 4speedtoploaders.com, is usually the top Google search result. David was kind enough to create the foreword for this effort. He answered all of my questions (even if they were basic) and provided solid contributions and direction. He also contributed drawings and photographs from his vast Toploader collection. If you need anything involving a Toploader, he is your man. Thank you, David.

Paul Cangialosi, a fellow CarTech author, also helped by answering questions and providing knowledge and direction. In fact, his book *How to Rebuild & Modify High-Performance Manual Transmissions* was a catalyst in creating demand for this dedicated Toploader book. A prolific specialist with many different manual transmission models, Paul is another go-to guy in the automotive world. Thank you, Paul.

A veritable wealth of information was available from Bob Mannel, the author of the book *Mustang & Ford Small Block V8: 1962–1969*. His work was especially helpful in determining many of the HEH and RUG codes. If your Toploader has a small-block Ford in front of it, his book should be on your library shelf as a reference. Thank you, Bob.

David Randal was another great source, and credit for his photos can be seen throughout this book. He shadowed David Kee during Toploader disassembly and reassembly and took many of the great and highly detailed photos that builders need to see. Thank you, David.

James Smart contributed greatly. His clear photos helped explain the nuances of rebuilding a Toploader with plenty of great and revealing build and detail photos. Thank you, James.

Without exception, all of the experts whom I contacted were onboard with this book from the beginning. They all wanted a place to centralize Toploader information—once and for all. Their other aim was to disprove incorrect information that has been constantly repeated. When this happens, as Bob Mannel says, it's very difficult to override longtime falsehoods with the facts. Nevertheless, that was the aim herein, and any mistakes or omissions are mine alone.

Thanks to the many Toploader fans on both sides of the market for these iconic transmissions. Thanks to the many folks who wouldn't use anything but a Toploader in their machines. In addition, thanks to those individuals and companies that continue to fill the demand for parts, assemblies, and even turnkey Toploaders for those users. These are the people who are keeping Toploaders alive and viable in today's performance automotive world.

On the home front, my wife, Donne, was always a big help to keep me from burning out while writing the thousands of words that fill this book. My daughter, Nikki, also helped in pacing me to deal with the necessary deadlines. With my loved ones helping me stay fresh, this big writing project always remained fun. Thank you to the two most important people in my life.

Thanks to my seemingly endless list of "gearhead" buddies who kept me motivated by asking how it was going. They were rewarded with endless anecdotes about Toploaders (even the non-Ford guys)—even if they didn't want to hear them. Thanks, guys. Regular friends are included in this group. Folks who asked about the progress (or lack thereof) had a positive effect on this project.

Please enjoy this team effort, as plenty of love, devotion, and care went into it.

FOREWORD

By David Kee
Owner of David Kee Toploader Transmissions Inc.

As a teenager, I began working with my own cars, getting ready for when I could get a license. I took two years of diesel-mechanic training in high school. I always had Fords, and since I didn't have much money, they were mostly mid-1960s cars that needed to be rebuilt to remain roadworthy. I had a few GM vehicles, but I never figured them out as well as the Fords.

My Toploader venture began with a 1969 Mustang that I was attempting to reassemble. In 1998, I wanted a 4-speed Toploader but thought that it would be impossible to find one. I found one in a scrapyard when I tripped on the shift-lever shafts that were sticking out of the ground. The Toploader was three-quarters (or more) buried in the dirt. After digging it out, I bought it for $20. After taking it apart, I determined what it needed. On my search for parts, I found some common items but not everything that was required. That is when I had the idea to have those parts made, and I was eventually able to do so for the whole transmission.

Having built these transmissions for more than 20 years, it is clear that today's Toploader industry is still strong. Even with everything that is available to be used in its place, builders still choose to use Toploaders. Some of my customers bought their cars when they were brand new. Now, those customers are having them rebuilt to relive their youth. Some use the same transmission with some improvements. Some have switched from an automatic to a manual transmission now that they know what they want and can afford it. Other customers want these transmissions for racing. Any way that you look at it, Toploaders are here to stay.

Scan this QR code with your smartphone to view the David Kee Toploader Transmissions website (davidkeetoploaders.com).

Over the years, I have worked with numerous editors to create magazine articles about Toploaders. Those articles were usually about rebuilds, and many ended up like abbreviated chapters of what could have been a more descriptive book. I understood that they were just small articles and that I was limited in the amount of content that could be submitted. So, there was not always adequate space to contain all of the necessary information. This often created confusion for readers, and that confusion can cause problems during a rebuild. In addition, the articles did not include the Toploader's interesting and informative history. However, I contributed what I could so that the information was available.

When John Carollo first called me to ask for my help in writing this book, I laughed. I told him that people have been asking me to write a book about the Toploader transmission for the past five years. I never took on that book project because I was not in a position to write it myself.

Instead, I agreed to work with John to help him produce this book because it is needed for the automotive industry. I thought that a Toploader book would be awesome. I liked

David Kee keeps many factory parts on hand, including these original Toploader cases. In addition, he has designed many of the reproduced parts that are needed for a quality Toploader rebuild. (Photo Courtesy David Randal)

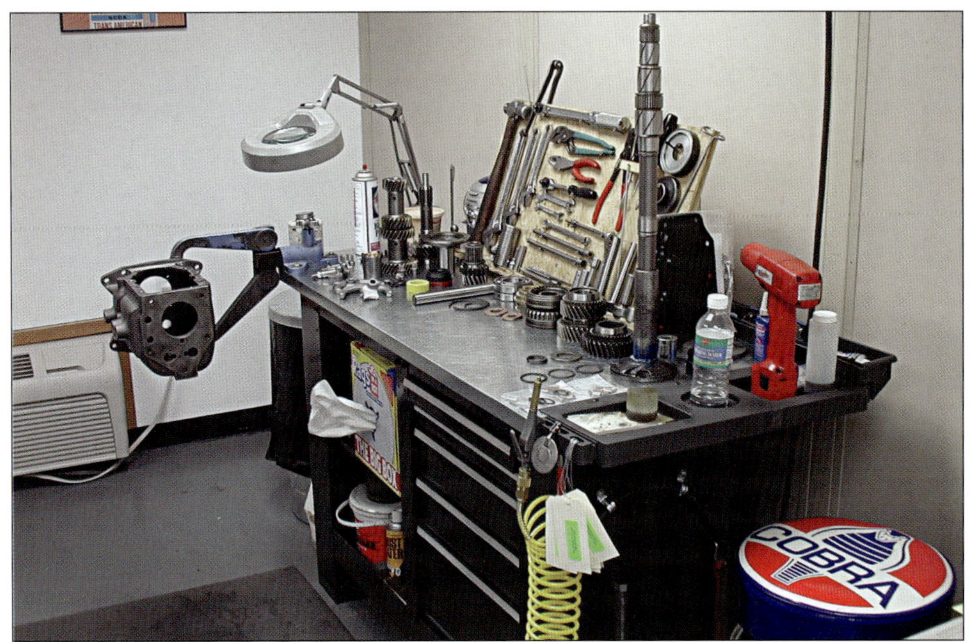

The bench of David Kee proves that it doesn't take much to create a good workspace for rebuilding a Toploader transmission. Note the small board of tools, the holding fixture that holds the case in the horizontal and vertical positions, and a place on the bench surface for parts that are ready to be installed. (Photo Courtesy David Randal)

the idea of having all of the Toploader information in one place. I tried to do just that on my website. Putting that information into accurate sequences and presenting nothing but correct information can make it easier to understand how Toploaders work and how they need to be disassembled and reassembled.

I also believe that all Toploader information should be as thorough as possible. The quality of a build can be seriously jeopardized when the details are left out. If a part is identified incorrectly, it's easy to unknowingly make a mistake. That mistake may evolve into something that may be a bigger and more costly problem after the cover has been bolted down.

A central place for complete Toploader information is needed, and that is the aim for this book.

Note from Author John Carollo:

Those in the performance world with an interest in Ford's Toploader 4-speed transmissions know that David Kee is the go-to guy for all things related to that topic. From hunting down the Toploader's elusive history to actually building them, David has spent many years deep inside their cast-iron cases. He created new and better parts and continues to supply a surprisingly large number of Toploader outlets around the world with the parts and information that are needed for rebuilds.

This re-creation of the full-size version of the 1/8-scale Monogram model car, The Big T, is on display at the Speedway Motors Museum of American Speed in Lincoln, Nebraska. Noted customizer Darryl Starbird designed the original model car and built a life-size version that was given to a lucky winner. (Photo Courtesy Jason Lubken, Speedway Motors Museum of American Speed)

From his shop in Texas, he has built thousands of Toploaders for many clients—from white-glove enthusiasts to hard-core racers. I pried him away from his workbench long enough to include his knowledge about Toploaders, which are his shop's one-and-only product.

After the winner took the full-size version of The Big T, it hasn't been seen again and remains missing to this day. Darryl Starbird worked with Predator Performance to re-create The Big T that is seen in these photos in the museum. David Kee built the Toploader 4-speed transmission that was used in this full-size re-creation. (Photo Courtesy Jason Lubken, Speedway Motors Museum of American Speed)

PREFACE

Why did I write another book about an original equipment manufacturer (OEM) transmission from the 1960s?

The answer is that Ford's Toploader 4-speed transmissions remain relevant today. As with many of the muscle car era's famous engines and their accompanying transmissions, Toploaders never fell out of favor. In fact, they have even grown in popularity.

Not long after muscle cars stopped being produced, their values began to appreciate. Saving these now-classic vehicles through restoration became a budding branch in the automotive aftermarket industry. Then, muscle cars were not only restored but went down a new and different path: they were hot rodded. Stock restorations and hot rod builds usually used the original transmissions and engines because their owners usually stayed loyal to the original manufacturer. Chrysler cars used Chrysler engines and transmissions. GM cars used GM engines and transmissions. So, what did Ford fans use? Blue Oval engines were almost always paired with a Toploader 4-speed when three pedals were the chosen format.

Toploaders made other performance inroads outside of the obvious muscle car category. In National Association for Stock Car Auto Racing (NASCAR), where the best OEM performance inventions were needed to last 500 grueling miles almost every weekend, Toploaders became the model that withstood the abuse. Later, Toploaders were redesigned (piece by piece), but the original basic style remained in use for years. The Jerico transmission became the standard in NASCAR and is still used in drag racing and road racing. These styles of 4-speeds use many of the Toploader's features, including the iconic opening on the top of the case.

Toploaders are still being used in the performance automotive world today, changing gears behind Ford engines in stock restorations and modified cars and trucks. So, many Toploaders are reborn into new kinds of cars. It is amazing that the 4-speed transmission that Ford introduced in

The Munster Koach*, as is depicted in this cartoon by artist Tom McClain, is one of the most iconic and popular cars from television. The "King of the Kustomizers," George Barris, built the original cars and equipped some of them with 4-speed Toploaders. (Illustration Courtesy Tom McClain)*

1964 is still relevant to enthusiasts, including many drivers who were born after 1964. The Toploader has spanned generations. However, this story doesn't end with the Toploader garnering new fans.

Today, engines from the 1960s use modern technology to be stronger and produce much higher output numbers than they did from the factory, as many surpass 1,000 hp. I can't help but wonder what the original Ford engineers and designers would have said in 1964 about bolting a 1,000-hp engine to their then-new Toploaders. To keep up with those bigger and better engines, the transmissions also had to be upgraded. Toploader transmissions have undergone that transition for two basic reasons.

First, the factory support and supply of parts ran out not long after Ford stopped installing them in production cars. That spawned cottage industries and loyal fans who took up the task of creating usable replacement parts and assemblies. They began by making the more commonly used (and abused) parts available for typical rebuilding tasks.

Second, businesses then made those replacement pieces even stronger and better. Along the way, visionaries used modern technology to better engineer their parts, better materials for more performance and reliability, and better machining for closer tolerances. A better overall product was created with each new part.

In addition, with all of the new technology being used, those new parts usually offer a better value too. The result is that it is possible to build a new and improved Toploader without having to chase down original factory parts. This means that almost every part of a Toploader has been faithfully reproduced for all types of users. In a still-evolving path, some of those parts are being designed as all-new pieces to handle the amazing load of two to three times the original horsepower numbers.

The primary purpose of this book is to collect all of today's facts on Toploaders, combine them with their rich history, and present it all in an understandable and useful manner. A lot goes on inside any transmission, so attention to detail is paramount. Each step of the disassembly, inspection, and reassembly has been broken down. There should be no doubt as to what is happening, the order in which the process takes place, and why and how it all fits together. With plenty of dedicated photos, many questions are answered and clarified.

However, that's not all. Part of this undertaking has been making a consistent use of the names for some parts. Over time, some parts have gained additional names, and that can be confusing for new and old Toploader fans. When needed, I included some of those alternate names and how they relate to the build.

The time to corral all of this new and old information is now. Loyal Toploader fans who want to rebuild or modify their Toploaders have more parts and information available to them than at any other time in Toploader and muscle car history. Of all the many wonderful horsepower gifts that the OEMs of Detroit bestowed upon gearheads, creating this book is the best way to honor a true muscle car icon: the Ford Toploader 4-speed transmission.

In addition to still being relevant today, this book was created because Toploaders are just plain cool. As evidence, George Barris, who is known as the "King of the Kustomizers," chose to use a Toploader transmission when he built the original *Munster Koach* hot rod in the 1960s for the popular TV series *The Munsters*. Reports vary if it was actually a 3-speed or 4-speed Toploader, but my research shows that at least some of the famous *Munster Koach* cars built by Barris at the time were 4-speed Toploaders. Much like George Barris's *Munster Koach,* the Toploader 4-speed lives on today, meeting new and old fans.

CHAPTER 1

History and Evolution

The decade of the 1960s was exciting for the performance cars of Detroit's Big Three manufacturers. Ford, General Motors, and Chrysler were engaged in what became the continued evolution and eventual peak of the distinctly American muscle car era.

The Early Days

In the early 1950s, engine displacement and power output increased because of two interesting and different influences. Cars were growing physically larger in size each model year, and this required larger engines and more power to move the newly increased mass. At the same time, postwar motorsports in the United States (at the organized and grassroots levels) was growing in popularity and incorporating stock-type cars with their more powerful engines. NASCAR was officially formed in 1949 with the intent of using brand-new, showroom-stock cars for oval-track racing. Two years later, the National Hot Rod Association (NHRA) was formed and began to organize drag racing competitions across the country.

Almost every racing association took advantage of Detroit's growing line of new overhead-valve (OHV) engines. Drivers across the country utilized the latest and greatest cars with bigger engines to win races. The trend worked, and fans packed the stands each week to see cars that looked just like theirs battle at their local tracks.

The car manufacturers quickly took note of what was occurring on NASCAR's dusty fairground dirt tracks and the NHRA's growing number of airstrips turned into drag strips. The fact that brand-new racing facilities were being created gave more credibility to this new racing movement. The factories fed engine evolution by designing special parts and programs with the goal of winning races, even if these efforts were sometimes underground, unofficial, or outright dark, backdoor programs.

With all of this growth, it wasn't long before all the manufacturers fully bought into the adage, "Win on Sunday; sell on Monday." Winning cars of all brands were shown in magazine and newspaper advertisements for the manufacturers, which touted their vehicles' performance and durability characteristics to car-buying readers. This snowball-like evolution helped fuel larger engines with more performance.

In 1950, the average automobile engine measured less than 200 ci. A mere 10 years later, that number increased to about 400 ci, and that was not the top end of the motor evolution in Detroit. The symbiotic relationship of needing a bigger engine for a bigger car played into using those bigger engines for racing. In addition, Detroit openly sold cars from the newly created angle of performance.

Factories began looking at other parts of the driveline to ensure that they were up to delivering the engine's increased horsepower to the racetrack's surface. As is proven constantly in racing, when a weak link fails, a stronger part is created. Soon, the original equipment manufacturers (OEMs) were upgrading not only engines but also transmissions and differentials to keep up with the rapidly evolving performance combinations. As racers sought more advantages, suspensions also received upgrades and began a new area for performance improvement and racing results.

The 1960s

With engine displacement increasing throughout the 1950s, the 1960s became the crescendo with sizes of 426, 427, 428, and 429 ci. Every step of the way, OEMs continued wringing the most out of those large powerplants. Carburetor, intake efficiency, and flow numbers were areas that yielded easy and quick improvements. The hot rod–termed "three Deuces" of the 1950s gave way to dual quads in the 1960s, delivering more air-and-fuel mixtures to bigger, more demanding engines that created even more horsepower.

Displacement in the 1960s for Ford grew to a maximum of 429 ci. NASCAR required 500 production units of a marque, so Ford commissioned Kar-Kraft to create the Boss 429 Mustang. All Boss 429s came with a Ford Toploader. (Photo Courtesy Wes Eisenschenk)

Right behind those engines, things were changing too. Despite numerous steady automatic transmission advances, manual transmissions were hands down the best and most popular for performance and racing. It came down to matching the engine's RPM to its maximum horsepower range on the street and track.

The Chevrolet Corvette is known as the first American sports car to use a 4-speed transmission, and it did so in 1957 with a BorgWarner T-10. This took the other OEMs by surprise because none of them had a 4-speed transmission of their own. To respond quickly and get this huge new improvement behind their best engines, the other OEMs quickly placed their orders for T-10s. Heading into the 1960s, the BorgWarner T-10 4-speed was the leader, and it was the only 4-speed.

Ford, General Motors, and Chrysler Create 4-Speed Transmissions

Behind the scenes in Detroit, even bigger engines were already quietly moving from the concept phase to drawing boards and prototype castings. They soon required strong transmissions (preferably 4-speeds) that could withstand more power and torque than ever before. The Big Three manufacturers had already done what they could to strengthen their own 3-speeds for more performance before turning to an outside vendor for T-10 4-speeds.

Still, it was obvious that 4-speeds had many advantages. The OEMs took the cue and began designing their own 4-speeds that were loosely based on the already-proven T-10. Chrysler prepared to launch its 426-ci Hemi engine, and Ford was creating its 427-ci engine. General Motors had several brands that were designing large engines. Chevy was ready to introduce its line of big-block engines that would also tout the now-magical 427-ci engine size. Pontiac had already released its 421-ci engine, and Buick and Oldsmobile had 400- and 394-ci engines, respectively. The big motors were coming, and each one would need a strong transmission.

The Big Three manufacturers introduced their own 4-speed transmissions around the same time: General Motors produced the Muncie 4-speed in 1963, Chrysler created the A-833 4-speed for the 1964 model year, and Ford designed what it called the Ford Design 4-speed for release in 1964.

These new factory 4-speeds arrived as the large 400-ci-plus engines were released to the public and the now-numerous racing sanctioning bodies. The buzz on the streets and tracks was huge. Bigger engines *and* a new 4-speed? Thousands of racers across the country were excited.

The Ford Design 4-Speed Transmission

According to most sources, the Ford Transmission and Chassis Division began designing what it called the Ford Design 4-speed transmission in late 1962. Toploader expert

David Kee noted that Ford component drawings for Toploader shift rails had a release date of November 1962. Another component drawing, this one for a Toploader detent, had a release date of May 1963. This lines up with Ford introducing the Toploader in 1964 in Galaxie models. Toploaders eventually came in three versions: 3-speeds, 4-speeds, and an overdrive model that was introduced in 1978. For this book, I am concentrating on the most popular of the series: the Ford Toploader 4-speed transmission that was used from 1964 to 1973.

Ford's new piece wasn't just a high-performance transmission that was designed for big Ford engines. The 4-speeds were the natural progression from 3-speed transmissions for all of the brands. They made for more efficient driving and even better gas mileage, which was not a major concern for performance-minded drivers but was very much so for fleet owners.

The Toploader became the go-to 4-speed that served a variety of Fords, Mercurys, and even some foreign models. It had a good run, beginning in 1964 and staying on Ford's active parts list through 1973, faithfully serving in 133 different models. Because of the 1970s' economic recession and gas crunch, the downsizing of many models brought in overdrive transmissions and smaller-displacement engines. A good example is the 1974 Mustang. All of this contributed to the end of the Toploader.

The Toploader was never replaced by a bigger and better performance version. By 1973, automatic transmissions had been even further developed and became more commonplace—even in trucks. The incorporation of overdrive helped make them even more desirable when gas prices increased. After 1973, Ford never made a 4-speed-only manual transmission of its own. However, it produced overdrive manual transmissions and outsourced some similar manual and performance transmissions.

The "Toploader" Nickname

The Toploader nickname came from the location of the single opening in the top of the transmission's case, where almost all of its internal parts are installed and serviced. While General Motors and Chrysler followed the style of the T-10 with its sole opening located on the driver's side of the case, the Ford powertrain engineers designed the Ford Design 4-speed transmission to use an opening that was on the top of the case.

This aspect of the Toploader design already had deep roots at Ford. The 3-speed transmission used in a Flathead-powered 1939 Ford was similar to the Toploader design, as the shifter came out of the top of the short, compact case. That transmission instantly became popular with hot rodders, racers, and other enthusiasts for its simplicity and durability. In very close variations, Ford's early 3-speed Toploader was used into the 1950s for Ford trucks, still bolted to the venerable and famous Flathead.

The new Toploader that followed 25 years later in 1964 offered the same traits to new generations of drivers who had much larger Ford engines. As this new transmission entered the realm of performance enthusiasts in the mid-1960s, users called it the Toploader, referring to the location of the access cover.

That cover placement yielded several distinct differences when it was compared to other transmissions. The most important difference was not making the shift rails and shifter forks move via openings in the cover. This eliminated any stress forces to

Toploader transmissions propelled Cobra Jet–powered cars, such as this 1973 Gran Torino Sport. This was the last year that a Toploader could be ordered from the factory in a Ford or Mercury muscle car. (Photo Courtesy Ken MacLean)

the cover when gears were engaged and under full torque. With this new design, the Toploader's case proved to be stronger, and many in the industry still say that it is the strongest of the 1960s' OEM 4-speeds.

Inside, the shifter forks work by using shift rails that are mounted into bosses that are part of the case's casting design. This provides a more complimentary range of motion than side-mounted designs for gears and synchronizers. In addition, the Toploader's design provided less drag and wear on connecting parts and tolerated faster power shifts. Both of these aspects were huge benefits for racing.

The strength of this case design is also shown by the cover that is used. With the structural and shifting forces now distributed evenly throughout a strong case and its components, the opening only needs a simple stamped sheet-metal cover. This cover doesn't need to contribute to the strength of the case. Its primary function is to basically retain the lubrication within the transmission while also acting as an access panel. The cover can be removed easily—to the point of being able to do so and have the transmission still operate. This is not the case for the side-loaded 4-speeds because removing their covers also removes and disconnects some of their internal components.

The validity of the Toploader's design is still true today, well over a half century later. Subsequent modern manual transmissions (performance or otherwise) also locate their openings at the top of the case. Some of today's notable, hard-core high-performance transmissions incorporated this idea with great success—to the point of having multiple access covers located on the top of the transmission. In some modern evolutions, the shifter engages its internal gears via that top opening. The relative ease of working on a manual transmission by using the opening at the top of the case makes everything from simple maintenance to a complete rebuild much easier.

Evolution

The Toploader experienced the typical evolution for a new transmission, which included growing pains. Ford was quick to provide speedy and excellent solutions for any issues. One of the most noted changes was an upgrade to the output shaft. Upon its debut, the fully synchronized 4-speed used a 25-spline output shaft that developed stress cracks where it met the driveshaft yoke spline. It was quickly discarded, and a larger-diameter, 28-spline shaft was the replacement. From there, Ford engineers improved it by using two new spline sizes based on the engine sizes with which they would be used. Engines of 260 to 390 ci used Toploaders with 28-spline output shafts. When Ford engines crested the 400-ci mark, beefy 31-spline output shafts were used for more strength. This solution worked, and no further problems were reported.

Another critical component, the input shaft, had two sizes for matching the two different engine-size groups. The standard input-shaft size of $1\frac{1}{16}$ inches in diameter was used in 260- to 390-ci engines. For bigger engines, a $1\frac{3}{8}$-inch-diameter input shaft was used. Today, descriptions for Toploaders often include the phrase "big in and big out" to describe having the bigger input and output shafts.

According to author Paul Cangialosi, the Toploader's $1\frac{3}{8}$-inch-diameter input shaft is the largest input shaft that was used in passenger-car 4-speed transmissions, as it was larger than Chrysler and GM's 1960s versions. That simple decision added even more to what became the Toploader's legacy of being the strongest of the factory 4-speeds. Both sizes of Toploader input shafts are 10 splines, so telling them apart visually is not easy. Another variation to note is that the smaller $1\frac{1}{16}$-inch input-shaft models were available in close- and wide-ratio

Although this Toploader looks like it is chrome, it is actually a modern Toploader with an aftermarket aluminum case and tailhousing that have been polished to look like chrome. (Photo Courtesy Ed Oetzel)

gear versions. In addition, Ford designated that transmissions with the 1³/₈-inch input shaft were only available as close-ratio units.

There is also the matter of how long the nose of the input shaft extends into the pilot bushing/bearing in the crankshaft. Input shafts that were used on small-blocks have a 1¼-inch nose, while big-block engines used an input shaft with a 3/4-inch nose (in length). Both sizes penetrate the pilot bushing/bearing 1/2 inch deep.

One more interesting evolution point of the Toploader is on the front of the main case, where the number of holes and bearing retainer sizes were upgraded. Toploaders built in that first year of 1964 had a four-hole pattern on the case around a smaller outside-diameter bearing retainer. That was quickly upgraded in 1965, when a bigger and stronger eight-hole pattern also incorporated a larger outside-diameter bearing retainer.

Benefits

With all Toploader gears except reverse being in constant interface, gears can be easily shifted up and down, engaging via synchronizer sleeves instead of sliding gears. Coupled with Ford's use of helical gears, this allows for faster shifts and, better yet, reduces the hard clashing of gears during those shifts.

The reverse sliding gear is a spur design located on the reverse idler. When reverse is engaged, the sliding gear is moved forward to couple with the straight-cut-gear teeth on the exterior of the first/second-gear synchronizer sleeve and turns the output shaft and driveshaft in reverse.

As with other 4-speeds coming from the OEMs, Toploaders were offered in wide- and close-ratio versions, which is important for performance-minded consumers. In fact, cars with 428 and 429 Ford engines were only available with close-ratio Toploaders. In wide-ratio versions, first gear was a 2.78:1 ratio, second was 1.93, third was 1.36, and fourth was 1.0. For close-ratio Toploaders, first gear was a 2.32:1 ratio, second was 1.69, third was 1.29, and fourth was the usual 1.0.

TECH TIP

Output-Shaft and Tailhousing Descriptions

Output shafts are described by the length of the transmission in which they fit, rather than the actual length of the output shaft. For example, a 24-inch-long transmission uses what is known as the 24-inch output shaft. The same is true for the other shafts that fit 25½- and 27-inch-long Toploaders.

Tailhousings are identified the same way. There is one notable difference, as the 25½-inch output shaft was only available as a 28-spline version. The 24- and 27-inch mainshafts were available in 28- and 31-spline versions. ■

Not Only for Muscle Cars

Ford wasn't only thinking "high-performance 4-speed" for its new transmission because attention-grabbing performance cars were only a small part of Ford's bottom line. Ford wanted its new transmission to work in a variety of platforms. To that end, Ford created the "modular" style.

Ford designed the case to be the standardized business end of the transmission and adjusted the tailhousings and output shafts for use in various cars. Subsequently, Toploaders came from Ford in three overall lengths: 24, 25½, and 27 inches. As the case was a uniform length of 10¹/₈ inches long, tailhousings came in three lengths: 14, 15½, and 17 inches to create those final three sizes. Output shafts also came in three different lengths to fit the three sizes of tailhousings.

The three transmission lengths were used in groups of cars, mostly according to their wheelbase/size, engine location, and shifter position inside the car. The 24-inch version (the shortest) was used on a mix of small cars: AC Cobras with 427 and 428 engines, Cougars, Falcons, Mustangs, and 1966–1967 Fairlanes and Mercury Comets. The next longer length (25½ inches) was used in the slightly larger 1964–1965 Fairlanes, Griffiths, Sunbeam Tigers, and TVRs. The longest version (27 inches) was used on full-size cars, such as Cyclones, Galaxies, 1968–1969 Fairlanes, Montereys, and Torinos.

In addition to being used with manual transmissions, Toploaders were engineered to precisely match the overall length of two of Ford's popular automatic transmissions. A 24-inch Toploader is the same length as a C-4 automatic. Ford's 27-inch Toploader is the same length as its C-6 automatic. This means that cars using these components can share the same driveshaft, reducing the number of parts and cost. From an enthusiast's perspective, it also means that swaps from one style to the other are accomplished easily and economically.

Bolted to Ford V-8s

Toploader 4-speeds were coupled with Ford V-8 engines of varying sizes. Beginning with Ford's famous 289-ci V-8, Toploader 4-speeds were used

In 1970, 7,014 Boss 302 Mustangs were produced, and all were equipped with Toploader transmissions. Grabber Blue (861) was the third-most-ordered color behind Competition Yellow (1,454) and Calypso Coral (866). (Photos Courtesy Wes Eisenschenk)

with the 260, 302, 351 Cleveland, 351 Windsor, 390, 410, 427, 428, and 429 engines (in no particular order). Ford fans are correct in noticing that Ford's 406 engine is not on this list.

The 406 engine in a 1962 Ford did not come with a 4-speed. Instead, the T-10 transmission was used. For 1963, the famous R Code model 427 Fords also used T-10s, as the Toploader was likely still in development at that time. By the time that Toploaders were ready to be fitted into full-size Galaxies, the 406 had already been dropped from production in favor of the new 427.

Afterlife and Living Onward

After the 4-speed Toploader's factory use stopped in 1973, it continued on the same path in the performance world because Ford enthusiasts still saw it as the only transmission to use. Much like many of the better OEM performance pieces of those muscle car days, new generations of replacement parts were produced for the Toploader. Big and small companies produced newer and better parts from the original designs. Only now, "better" meant a newer design, and the metallurgy and machining processes could be improved. Soon, many of these new pieces were better than the originals, providing performance results that could only have been dreamt of in the 1970s.

Starting with stouter-yet-lighter aluminum cases and tailhousings, improved gearsets, synchronizers, and shafts have been reproduced as stronger-than-ever pieces. As the replacement-parts list grew, it became more complete. Today, except for the longer tailhousings that are not used as much, one can build a Toploader without being limited to chasing down original parts.

Muscle cars can be painstakingly restored or upgraded for maximum performance. The Toploader lives on today because it works for stock restorations and performance builds. Improved parts and assemblies are available for those looking to take advantage of the design and performance of Ford's Toploader 4-speed transmission, which was one of the best ever to be made.

IDENTIFICATION

Toploaders came from the factory with several indicators that reveal their identity. Now, more than 60-plus years removed from being installed in cars at the factory, and with more than 130 different Toploader versions in existence, some of these identification keys should be taken with a grain of salt when they are found. The problem is that there is no way to guarantee if any particular Toploader is still in factory condition when it is found.

From routine maintenance to slapped-together repairs and outright deception, parts can be easily changed. The overall simplicity of the Toploader's design made changing those parts relatively easy. So, assume nothing until all of the indicators and specifications on the transmission have been listed, studied, and confirmed. If all of the markers for identifying a Toploader line up correctly, one can assume that transmission, at the very least, matches factory specifications. To identify 4-speed Toploaders, I solely use the factory information and specifications.

First and foremost, Toploader 3-speed transmissions are often misidentified as 4-speeds. A quick way to identify a 3-speed Toploader is by the number of the top cover's 1/2-inch bolts. The 4-speeds have 10 top-cover bolts and 3-speeds have 9.

Understanding a Toploader's History

Gathering historic data about the 4-speed Toploader is an ongoing process. After this book goes to print, a page or two from the 1960s or 1970s could surface and affect this data. It's something that we all must accept.

The bottom line is that you must have confirmation regarding all of the critical indicators and information before ordering parts for replacement or upgrading. Establishing the correct model/year is critical because typical internal evolutionary changes can include and affect a number of components. Over the years, various shift rails, detents, gear ratios (including the cluster gear and speedometer gear), upgrades, etc. were used and updated in Toploaders. The speedometer gear is a good example of a small change that makes a difference. Speedometer gears changed from having six teeth to seven teeth and then to eight teeth. Those three changes were noted in tag codes.

Tag Codes

The most common and basic method to identify a 4-speed Toploader is the metal tag that is riveted to the front passenger's side of the case. First, look how the tag is mounted to the case. From the factory, a simple, round-head metal rivet was used to secure the metal tag to the case. If a screw or bolt is used, this may indicate a swapped tag. Keeping that in mind, move on to the code on the tag.

Toploader tags have HEH or RUG prefixes that are followed by suffixes of one or more letters or numbers. Ford used alphabetical order from A through Z on the suffixes and purposely left out the letters I, O, and Q. This reduced the chance that they could easily be mistaken for the numbers 1 and 0.

While the letters may be alphabetically in order, tag codes are not in any chronological order. One suffix may line up with one year and the next suffix may jump forward or backward several years. Ford's use of HEH codes was used from its inception until about 1967. I used the word "about" because some RUG codes also connect to 1967 models. So, don't

Unfortunately, many code tags look like this. Being on the outside of the case, they are subjected to road debris and grime. The good news is that Ford anticipated this and used raised-letter stamping, which makes them easier to read. (Photo Courtesy David Randal)

Part of a good rebuild is making the code tag easily readable, such as this RUG-code tag. This provides a clear view to match up a number of factors to confirm a Toploader's specifications and true identity. (Photo Courtesy David Kee)

Finding an intact code tag is always promising for identification. Wise Toploader hunters and builders know that this is only the first of many steps. The goal is to identify the specifications regarding gear ratios, the number of splines, and the vehicle in which it was used.

rely on any one indicator for a final and positive identification. I listed the tag codes in alphabetical order (in the following charts) in two groups for ease of reading when matching up the letters. From these tag codes, the year, vehicle, engine size, transmission ratio, and spline count can be decoded.

Ford created more RUG labels than HEH designations. HEH codes were generally used only in the two years of 1964 and 1966. RUG codes were generally used in the seven years from 1967 to 1973.

The only exception to this was for the Fairlane 427 in 1966, which used the HEH-CJ code. That same code was carried over into 1967 models before being replaced by RUG-L.

I leaned heavily on experts to compile the most up-to-date list. There are missing pieces on this list because it is ever evolving. I attempted to keep errors to a minimum and left descriptors blank when I could not confirm a specification. David Kee has compiled his listing showing the various combinations seen in Toploaders over the years. It contains more than 100 HEH and RUG codes that show the many applications where Toploaders were used.

I also included the work of Bob Mannel, who wrote *Mustang & Ford Small Block V8: 1962–1969*. His work detailing the listings that Ford paired with its small-blocks (and a few big-blocks) is very detailed and highly recommended. Together, these two experts have determined nearly all of the codes, and they even shot down a few questionable codes that have been allowed to exist. At the very least, the codes that have been accepted for years but never really had any confirmation to back them up are explained.

Ford used this transmission in many vehicles, so paying close attention to all of the indicators when trying to identify a Toploader is very important to produce the correct results. For example, in 1964, the first year that Ford began installing the Toploader into its vehicles, there were 11 applications. Three years later, there were up to 25 applications. The letter combinations do not match up to any chronological order. Another thing to remember is that close-ratio transmissions often have 31 splines—but not always. There are some 28-spline, close-ratio Toploaders.

There is usually a series of numbers below the RUG and HEH codes on the metal tags. These are succession numbers, and they indicate how many of that particular model number were created. The confusing part is that Ford didn't begin the number sequence with zero. Instead, it began with 010001. The result is a number that may read something like "024043." Also, these numbers do not pertain to the serial number of the vehicle in which the transmission was installed.

Lastly, Ford's practice was to use wide-ratio Toploaders with its standard-power engines while close-ratio versions were installed behind its performance engines. Close-ratio examples included the 289 HiPo, 390 4-V, and 427. Others usually bolted up to wide-ratio units. It's best to try to determine which engine came with the Toploader that is being identified. The information could help to sort out the many factors to identify and confirm a Toploader's identity.

HEH Toploaders

In 1965, Ford began printing tags with two-letter suffixes. Often, the two-letter tags replaced previous single-letter tags on 4-speeds. Speedometer gear differences and evolution also showed up on some listings.

Examples of Verified Progression through 1965

- HEH-J (6-tooth speedometer gear) to HEH-BL (7-tooth speedometer gear) to HEH-CC (change in all outer shift levers)
- HEH-K (6-tooth speedometer gear) to HEH-BM (7-tooth speedometer gear) to HEH-CD (change in all outer shift levers)
- HEH-L (7-tooth speedometer gear) to HEH-BN (8-tooth speedometer gear)
- HEH-M (7-tooth speedometer gear) to HEH-BP (8-tooth speedometer gear, 25 splines) to HEH-BS (28 splines)
- HEH-P (7-tooth speedometer gear) to HEH-BR (8-tooth speedometer gear, 25 splines) to HEH-BT (28 splines)
- HEH-R to HEH-CB (change in all outer shift levers)

HEH Notes

HEH-C is not fully confirmed. It was used in a 1964 Comet with a 289 HiPo engine. The ratio for this car has not been determined or confirmed. Similarly equipped Safari Comets use close-ratio Toploaders. Since I could not confirm the HEH-C code, Bob Mannel, author of the book *Mustang & Ford Small Block V8: 1962–1969*, suspects that it might be for the 1964 Comet 289 HiPo Toploader that was used in a Comet with a 289-4V engine but with a 1964-era, 25-spline output shaft. The 289 HiPo torque would have exceeded the torque capacity of that shaft, so that would not have been the shaft that was used. Mercury (and Ford) would have to come up with a unique 28-spline output shaft, which would have created a unique code.

HEH Single-Letter Suffixes

Tag	Year	Vehicle	Engine	Ratio	Comments
HEH-A	1964	Comet/Falcon	260	Wide	25 spline
HEH-B	1964	Meteor/Fairlane	289-2V	Wide	28 spline
HEH-C	1964	Comet	289 HiPo	Wide	25 spline
HEH-D	1964	Galaxie/Monterey	390	Close	28 spline
HEH-E	1964 1964–1967	Meteor/Fairlane, Sunbeam Tiger	289-4V 289 HiPo	Close	25½-inch transmission, 28 spline
HEH-F	1964	Monterey	390-2V	Wide	28 spline
HEH-G	1964	Mustang	260, 289-4V	Wide	Before August 20, 1964, 25 spline
HEH-H	1964	Galaxie/Monterey	427-4V/8V	Close	28 spline
HEH-J	1965	Galaxie/Monterey	390-4V	Close	28 spline
HEH-K	1965	Monterey	390-2V	Wide	28 spline
HEH-L	1965	Fairlane	289-2V/4V	Wide	25½-inch trans, 28 spline
HEH-M	1964	Falcon, Comet	289-2V, 289-2V/4V	Wide	25 spline
HEH-N	1965	Fairlane	289 HiPo	Close	25½-inch transmission, 28 spline
HEH-P	1964	Mustang	289-2V/4V	Wide	25 spline August 20, 1964, to December 30, 1964
HEH-R	1965	Galaxie/Monterey	427-8V	Close	28 spline
HEH-S	1964½	Mustang	289 HiPo	Close	Before August 20, 1964
HEH-T	1965	Mustang	289 HiPo	Close	From August 20, 1964, to October 1, 1964, 28 spline
HEH-U	1964	Comet	289 HiPo	Unconfirmed	28 spline

HEH Dual-Letter Suffixes					
Tag	Year	Vehicle	Engine	Ratio	Comments
HEH-AM	1966	Galaxie	427-8V	Close	31 spline
HEH-AR	1966	Comet/Fairlane	390-2V/4V	Close	28 spline
HEH-AT	1965	Galaxie	427	Close	28 spline
HEH-BK	1965	Comet	289 HiPo	Close	28 spline
HEH-BL	1965	Galaxie/Monterey	390-4V	Close	28 spline
HEH-BM	1965	Monterey	390-2V	Wide	From December 1, 1964, to April 1, 1965, 28 spline
HEH-BN	1965	Fairlane	289-2V/4V	Wide	After December 1, 1964, 28 spline
HEH-BP	1965	Falcon Comet	289-2V 289-2V/4V	Wide	From October 1, 1964, to February 1, 1965, 28 spline
HEH-BR	1965	Mustang	289-2V/4V	Wide	From December 30, 1964, to February 1, 1965, 28 spline
HEH-BS	1965	Falcon Comet	289-2V 289-2V/4V	Wide	After February 1, 1965, 28 spline
HEH-BT	1965	Mustang	289-2V/4V	Wide	From February 1, 1965, 28 spline
HEH-BV	1966	Comet/Fairlane/ Falcon	289-2V	Wide	28 spline
HEH-BW	1966	Mustang	289-2V/4V	Wide	28 spline
HEH-BX	1965–1966	Mustang	289 HiPo	Close	From October 1, 1964, 28 spline
HEH-BY	1965	AC Cobra	427	Close	28 spline
HEH-CB	1965	Galaxie	427-8V	Close	28 spline
HEH-CC	1965–1966	Galaxie	390-4V	Close	28 spline
HEH-CD	1965	Monterey	390-2V	Wide	28 spline
HEH-CF	1965, 1967	TVR/Griffith, Sunbeam Tiger	289-2V/4V, 289-2V	Wide	25½-inch transmission, 28 spline
HEH-CG	1966	Galaxie, Monterey	428-4V, 410/428-4V	Close	31 spline
HEH-CJ	1967	Fairlane	427-8V	Close	31 spline
HEH-CL	1966	Comet/Fairlane	390GT-4V	Wide	28 spline
HEH-CT	1966	Galaxie	427	Close	31 spline

It cannot be determined if there actually was an HEH-C or that package just never had a unique code. Remember, 1964 Comet 289 HiPo engines with 4-speeds were only offered for the last four months of 1964 production, and they were only available by special order. This could cause long waits for vehicle delivery. The HEH-C code continues to be a mystery. Was it an actual tag from a 1964 Comet 289 HiPo, or was it from a 1965 Comet 289 HiPo? Toploader and Ford experts are still searching for the answer.

HEH-U is also not fully confirmed. It was said to be used in a 1964 Comet with a 289-hp engine and a 28-spline, 4-speed Toploader. Confirming if this code was for a wide- or close-ratio unit was difficult, much less determining the existence of such a code. I checked with Bob Mannel, who provided this information. This car and driveline combination was created for a 40-day durability test and was updated from a 3-speed to the new Toploader in 1964. Mercury also built 10 similar cars in April 1964 for an African Safari Rally, and they were likely equipped the same way.

There is no code for HEH-U in any of Mannel's extensive Ford or Mercury documents. In addition, there is a shortage of literature on HP Mercury Comets produced by Ford for the 1964–1965 model year, and Mercury's build records are not as plentiful as Ford's. Mannel's research could not confirm this HEH-U model as being a close-ratio unit, even though that would have been the logical choice for such a build. He, too, thought it would be a close-ratio unit, but as of going to print, I have not confirmed that it is wide ratio or close ratio. Mannel suggested that it could also be a 1965 Comet 289 HiPo with a close-ratio unit. He also pointed out that the HEH-U code was quite far down the HEH list—possibly too far down to have come from a 1964–1965 model.

Regarding which ratio was used for an HEH-U application, Mercury would likely not have used a wide-ratio unit with the 289 HiPo, as Ford never did. Magazine articles confirmed that the March 26–30, 1964, Safari Comets being prepped for that rally had Toploaders with close-ratio units. This was just before Mercury released its 1964 Technical Service Bulletin (TSB) 3A, dated April 17, 1964, which stated that the Comet 289 HiPo was now available with the Toploader 4-speed. This was early in the year and increases the likelihood that Mercury used the same 4-speed in the Safari and special-order Comets with the 289 HiPo engine and 4-speed.

Another factor is that the Mustang received the 289 HiPo in June 1964 and had the 28-spline Toploader that was the same as the those used on the Safari Comets. The code for that combination was HEH-S. The suffix letter may seem a little out of order in the alphabet, but that was because the Mustang was titled as a 1965 model, despite being built on the assembly line of 1964 Fairlanes. The only difference between the HEH-S and HEH-T was the front of the case. The "S" had only the original narrow, four-bolt pattern while the "T" had both the narrow and wide, eight-bolt patterns. This was a distinction between all 1964 Toploaders (narrow pattern) and 1965 Toploaders (both narrow and wide patterns) and is why the codes changed from 1964 to 1965.

The Comet 289 HiPo has yet to be verified, except for HEH-BK in 1965. This has been verified by several owners of 1965 Comet HiPo vehicles, although the HEH-BK code is not listed in any Ford or Mercury literature. Photos of tags were provided to Bob Mannel for his records. HEH-BK was likely a successor to HEH-U, but that is unconfirmed.

With the Safari Comets using close-ratio, 28-spline Toploaders, many believe that all 1964 Comets with 289 HiPo engines received the same ratio of transmission for the 4-speeds. With a 3.89:1 rear gear (the same gear ratio as the Fairlane 289 HiPo with the close-ratio Toploader), the close-ratio unit would be almost a necessity to keep the engine in its target RPM range for optimal performance. Although documentation has not yet confirmed it, Bob Mannel estimated that the chance for all 1964 Comet 289 HiPo vehicles getting close-ratio Toploaders was about 99.99 percent.

Mannel could find no documentation of the existence of an HEH-AT tag code. It's been reported as a 1965 Galaxie 427 close-ratio unit with a 28-spline output shaft. This could be one of those questionable listings that has been widely circulated and is being accepted as true. For comparison, HEH-AM lists a 1966 Galaxie with a 427-8V close-ratio unit and a 31-spline output-shaft package. This is another example of where experts are still searching for the truth.

Some of Mannel's information came from Master Parts Catalogs. He said that there are occasional errors, but they are rare. Mannel suggested that dates should be considered only as a guide because no one knows whether the date in question was confirmed as a release date, assembly date, or delivery date.

In 1964 (1964½), the 260-2V, 289-4V, and 289 HiPo (late June 1964) were listed for the Mustang. Toploader 4-speeds were not available for the 260-2V Mustang—only the 289-4V and 289 HiPo were available. However, in late 1964 production, Toploaders were used behind 260-2V Falcons and Comets.

Model Changes with Toploaders

Ford and Mercury changed platform model names as their cars evolved. Overall, Galaxies were full-size Fords. Montereys were full-size Mercurys. Fairlanes were intermediate-size Fords. Falcons were Ford's compact car from 1964 to 1965 and its shortened intermediate car from 1966 to 1969. Although they were still considered to be compact cars after 1966, there were actually shortened versions of the intermediates—they used the same 4-speeds and were grouped with the intermediates. Comets were Mercury's compact car from 1964 to 1965 and its intermediate car from 1966 to 1969. Mustangs and Cougars are also called pony cars. Mavericks, which debuted in 1970, never came with a Toploader.

Displacements from 1965 to 1969 were 410, 427, 428, and 429, and all used big input shafts and 31-spline output shafts. However, there was an exception in 1969, where a 351/390-4V also received a small input shaft and 31-spline output shaft. The 1964½–1965 Galaxie used a big input shaft with a 28-spline output shaft.

The 410 Mercury engine was created in 1965 and was used exclusively in 1966–1968 full-size Mercury, Monterey, Park Lane, and Colony Park vehicles. This engine was considered an FE model and had 345 hp and 475 ft-lbs of torque. It was created with a stroke of 3.70 inches and a bore of 4.20 inches. It was not related to the MEL engine of the late 1950s with the same displacement size.

RUG Toploaders

The other Toploader tag prefix is RUG, which is more common than HEH. The RUG code was used on the majority of 4-speed Toploaders, as it was used for seven years (1967–1973), while the HEH code was only used for three years (1964–1966). Some RUG codes used a number after the suffix to differentiate similar models.

Case Codes

The 4-speed Toploader cases were made with two different bolt patterns for attachment to the bell-

RUG-A through RUG-V1					
Tag	Year	Vehicle	Engine	Ratio	Comments
RUG-A	1967	Galaxie/Monterey	390-24/4V	Close	28 spline
RUG-A1	1967	Galaxie/Monterey	390-24/4V	Close	28 spline
RUG-A2	1967	Galaxie/Monterey	390-24/4V	Close	28 spline
RUG-AD	1968	Cougar/Mustang	390GT-4V	Close	28 spline
RUG-AD1	1969	Cougar/Mustang	390-4V	Close	28 spline
RUG-AE	1968	Cougar/Mustang	428-4V	Close	31 spline
RUG-AE1	1968–1969	Cougar/Mustang	428-4V	Close	31 spline
RUG-AE2	1969	Cougar/Mustang	428,429-4V, Boss 429	Close	31 spline
RUG-AF	1968	Comet/Fairlane	428-4V	Close	31 spline
RUG-AG	1969	Cougar/Mustang Mustang	302-2V, 351-2V/4V	Close	28 spline
RUG-AH	1969	Comet/Fairlane	351-2V	Close	28 spline
RUG-AJ	1969	Comet/Fairlane	428	Close	31 spline
RUG-AK	1969	Comet/Fairlane	351-4V	Close	31 spline
RUG-AL	1969	Comet/Fairlane	390-4V	Close	28 spline
RUG-AR	1970	Fairlane	351	Close	28 spline
RUG-AR1	1971	Fairlane	351	Close	28 spline
RUG-AS	1970	Fairlane	351	Close	31 spline
RUG-AS1	1970	Fairlane	351	Close	31 spline
RUG-AT	1970	Fairlane	351	Close	28 spline
RUG-AT1	1970	Fairlane	351	Close	28 spline
RUG-AU	1970	Fairlane	429	Close	31 spline
RUG-AU1	1970–1971	Torino	429	Close	31 spline
RUG-AV	1970	Mustang	302, 351, Boss 302	Wide	28 spline
RUG-AV1	1970–1971	Mustang	302-4V, 351-4V	Wide	28 spline
RUG-AW	1970	Mustang	302, 351, Boss 302	Close	28 spline
RUG-AW1	1970–1971	Mustang	302-4V, 351-4V	Close	28 spline
RUG-AZ	1970	Mustang	428 CJ, Boss 429	Close	31 spline
RUG-AZ1	1971	Mustang	429-4V	Close	31 spline
RUG-B	1967	Galaxie	427-8V	Close	31 spline
RUG-B1	1967	Galaxie	427-8V	Close	31 spline
RUG-B2	1967	Galaxie	427-4V	Close	31 spline
RUG-BA	1970	Fairlane	351	Wide	28 spline
RUG-BA1	1970–1971	Fairlane	351-4V	Wide	31 spline
RUG-BF	1972	Fairlane	351	Wide	Before December 1, 1971, 28 spline

RUG-A through RUG-V1					
Tag	**Year**	**Vehicle**	**Engine**	**Ratio**	**Comments**
RUG-BF1	1972	Fairlane	351	Wide	After December 1, 1971, 28 spline
RUG-BG	1972	Fairlane/Torino	351	Wide	Before December 1, 1971, 31 spline
RUG-BG1	1972	Torino	351	Wide	After December 1, 1971, 31 spline
RUG-BG2	1973	Torino	351	Wide	31 spline
RUG-BJ	1971	Mustang	351 CJ, Boss 351	Wide	Before December 1, 1971, 28 spline
RUG-BJ1	1972	Mustang	351 CJ, Boss 351	Wide	After December 1, 1971, 28 spline
RUG-C	1967–1969	Comet/Fairlane	390-2V/4V	Close	Except GT, 28 spline
RUG-C1	1967–1969	Comet/Fairlane	390-2V/4V	Close	Except GT, 28 spline
RUG-C2	1967–1969	Comet/Fairlane	390-2V/4V	Close	Except GT, 28 spline
RUG-D	1967–1969	Comet/Fairlane, Falcon	289-2V, 289-2V/4V	Wide	28 spline
RUG-D1	1967	Fairlane/Falcon, Falcon	289-2V, 289-2V/4V	Wide	28 spline
RUG-D2	1967/69, 1969	Comet Fairlane Falcon Comet/Fairlane	289-2V, 302-2V/4V 289/302-2V 289-2V/4V 351-2V	Wide	28 spline
RUG-E	1967–1968	Cougar/Mustang	289-2V/4V	Wide	28 spline
RUG-E1	1967–1968	Cougar/Mustang	289-2V/4V	Wide	28 spline
RUG-E2	1967–1968	Cougar/Mustang	289-2V, 302-4V	Wide	28 spline
RUG-E3	1969	Mustang, Cougar/ Mustang	302-2V, 351-2V/4V	Wide	28 spline
RUG-G	1967	Galaxie	428-4V	Close	31 spline
RUG-G1	1967	Galaxie Monterey	428-4V 410/428-4V	Close	31 spline
RUG-G2	1967	Galaxie Monterey	428-4V 410/428-4V	Close	31 spline
RUG-J	1967	Comet/Fairlane	390-4V GT	Wide	28 spline
RUG-J1	1967	Comet/Fairlane	390-4V GT	Wide	28 spline
RUG-J2	1968–1969	Comet/Fairlane	390-4V GT	Wide	28 spline
RUG-L	1967	Comet/Fairlane	427-4V/8V	Close	31 spline
RUG-L1	1967	Comet/Fairlane	427-4V/8V	Close	31 spline
RUG-L2	1967	Comet/Fairlane	427-4V/8V	Close	31 spline
RUG-M	1967	Cougar/Mustang	390-4V	Wide	28 spline
RUG-M1	1967	Cougar/Mustang	390-4V	Wide	28 spline
RUG-M2	1968	Cougar/Mustang	390GT-4V	Wide	28 spline
RUG-M3	1969	Cougar/Mustang	390-4V	Wide	28 spline
RUG-N	1967	Mustang	289 HiPo	Close	28 spline
RUG-N1	1967	Mustang	289 Hipo	Close	28 spline
RUG-N2	1968	Cougar/Mustang	289 HiPo	Close	28 spline
RUG-N3	1968	Mustang	289	Close	28 spline
RUG-S	1968	Mustang GT500	428	Close	31 spline
RUG-T	1968	Galaxie, Monterey	390-4V, 390-2V/-4V	Wide	28 spline
RUG-V	1968	Galaxie	428-4V	Close	31 spline
RUG-V1	1969	Galaxie	429-4V	Close	31 spline

Case codes are mostly found at the top of the passenger's side of the case near the cover. Ford had some casting numbers on the driver's side in the same location on a few models. Case codes C4AR and C5AR are found on the driver's side, as this photo shows. Ford put codes C8AR and D2AR on the passenger's side. There were two versions of the D2AR case, and both case codes are on the passenger's side. There was a total of five iterations of cases made from those four prefixes with a total of seven variations used. (Photo Courtesy David Randal)

housing. The early-model case had four bolt holes on the front, and later models had eight. Ford wanted to make a stronger connection between the transmission and bellhousing. During the rest of the production run of the Toploader, Ford made only a few subtle changes to the newer-style main cases.

Looking at the cases from the front or bellhousing side, differences between the two styles are easily noticeable. The early main case bolt pattern of 1964 is more rectangular and is known for having only four bolt holes. Overall, it was only used for one year, and there are fewer of these cases than those from 1965 to 1973.

On the later models, eight bolt holes were distributed in an hourglass shape on the front of the case. Interchangeability between the two styles was continued because both styles of cases use the same bolt pattern for the inner four holes. The four additional holes in a larger expanse of the flange provided more strength for the driveline parts that face the twisting forces of torque.

To illustrate how providing more strength to certain areas adds to the overall strength of the case, modern aftermarket cases also have a thicker flange for bolting to the bellhousing. This helps in general but it also adds significantly to the strength value when the components are cast of aluminum.

The two Ford cases look almost identical from the sides, even though a few slight changes were made in the 1968–1971 cases and again in the 1972 cases. The changes made to the sides of the cases are very subtle.

The casting numbers of the cases are below. The "RF" prefix stands for "Rough Finish." This same code is used on some tailhousings.

Some of the last D2 casting cases had the front boss machined and threaded for a high-gear timing retard for California vehicle emissions. These were located on the driver's side at the very front of the case and

Case Codes

Casting Number	Comments
C4AR-7006-A	1964 casting; almost certainly used with narrow, four-hole case
RF C4AR-7003-A	1964 casting; used in 1964 with narrow, four-hole case
RF C5AR-7006-D	1965 casting used from 1965 to 1967; wide, eight-hole case
RF C8AR-7006-D	1968 casting used from 1968 to 1971; wide, eight-hole case
RF D2AR-7006-CA	1972 casting in late 1971; wide, eight-hole case
RF-D2AR-7006-CB	1972 casting used from 1972 to 1973; wide, eight-hole case
D2AR7006-G	1972–1973 casting; most likely used with wide, eight-hole case

Ford made 31 different sizes and styles of tailhousing castings. They fit multiple car platforms, three different transmission lengths, and assorted shifter locations. These six models show some of the differences in length and shifter-mounting locations. (Photo Courtesy David Randal)

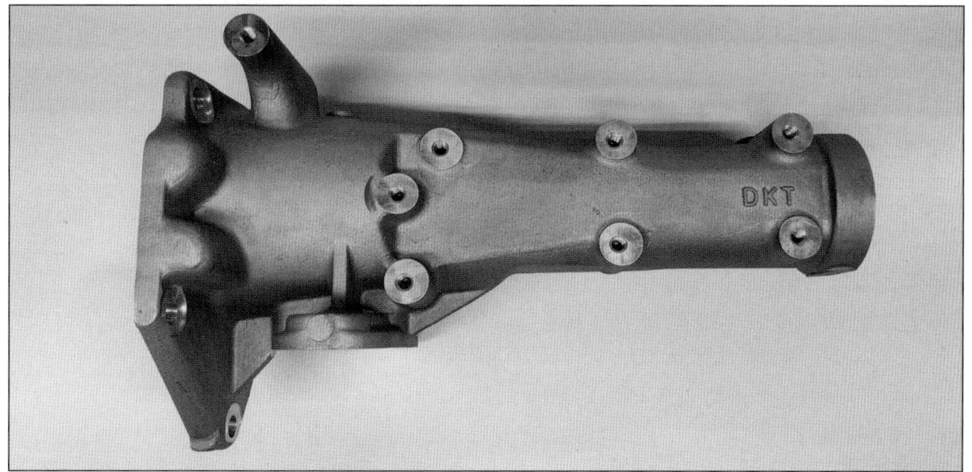

This aftermarket tailhousing from David Kee Toploader Transmissions, shows the simplicity and evolution of a Toploader's tailhousing. It's made from cast aluminum but does not sacrifice strength for weight reduction. Note the thicker flange where it bolts up to the case. (Photo Courtesy David Kee)

in line with the third/fourth gear shifter rail. On the same-year cases, many confuse the switch above the detent set screws on the driver's side of the case to be a reverse-light switch. Instead, it is a switch used to activate a seat-belt light on the dash if the transmission was shifted to any gear and the driver's seat belt was not fastened.

The XAA 12512/ALCOA 2 factory aluminum case was used in 1969–1970 factory road racing applications to reduce weight. Very few of these cases were made. Most estimates say that as few as 10 were created.

Tailhousing Codes

Toploaders were available from Ford in three overall lengths (24, 25½, and 27 inches long) to accommodate more than 133 applications. With all of the cases being the same length, tailhousing applications can be used in cars of various wheelbases with various overall transmission lengths and shifter mounting points. Therefore, Toploader tailhousings were available in three lengths to accomplish this: 14, 15½, or 17 inches.

The output shafts inside were also available in three different lengths to fit the three tailhousing sizes, but I am concentrating on identifying tailhousings at this point. Also, the changes for length and positioning of the shifter are about the only differences to these pieces. They all mounted the same with five bolts, used the same rear bearing and seal, and were made of cast iron. As far as any Toploader historian knows, Ford never made any aluminum tailhousings, although aftermarket aluminum tailhousings are now available.

The 31 different applications of Ford Toploader tailhousings used an identification system that began with a letter and then used numbers and letters to differentiate between models and equipment. For establishing a Toploader's identity, use the tailhousing code, it's length, and which spline is used to match up with the engine size. The "RF" prefix code stands for "Rough Finish." This code appears to be used only on the longest tailhousings that were installed in full-size cars.

Tailhousing Codes	
Code	**Use/Notes**
C4AR-7A040 A	1964–1967 Galaxie, 289, 390, except 427/428; 17-inch length; 28 spline
C4DR-7A040 A	1964–1965 Comet/Falcon; front shifter mounting holes drilled and tapped; 14-inch length; 25 or 28 spline
C4DR-7A040 A	1964–1973 Cougar/Mustang; rear shifter mounting holes drilled and tapped, and front lower shifter mounting pads milled off; 14-inch length; 25 or 28 spline
C4OR-7A040 A	1964–1965 Fairlane, Tiger, Griffin, and TVR; 15½-inch length; 28 spline
C4ZR-7A040-A	1964–1973 Cougar/Mustang 289, 302, 351; 14-inch length; 25 or 28 spline (only has rear pattern)
RF-C6AR-7A040-B	1966–1967 Galaxie 427, 428; 17-inch length; 31 spline
C60A-6394-D	390-4V after February 15, 1968, and all of 1968–1970 428 Cobra Jets
C6AR-7A040-B	1966–1967 Galaxie/Monterey 427/428
C6OR-7A040-C and C7OR-7A040-A	1966–1968 Cyclone/Fairlane/Ranchero/Torino 289, 302, 390; 1966–1969 Falcon 289, 302; 1966–1969 Cougar/Mustang 390; 14-inch length; 28 spline
C6OR-7A040-C and C7OR-7A040-A	1967–up Cyclone/Fairlane 427, 428; 1968–1969 Mustang 428, 429; 14-inch length; 31 spline
RF-C8AR-7A040-B	1966–1967 Galaxie 427, 428; 17-inch length; 31 spline
C6OR-7A040-C and C7OR-7A040-A	1966–1968 Cyclone/Fairlane/Ranchero/Torino 289, 302, 390; 1966–1969 Falcon 289, 302; 1966–1969 Cougar/Mustang 390; 14-inch length; 28 spline
C6OR-7A040-C and C7OR-7A040-A	1966–up Cyclone/Fairlane/Falcon 427, 428; 1968–1969 Mustang 428, 429; 14-inch length; machined for center shift pattern; 31 spline
C6OR-7A040-C	1966 Mustang (machined for rear shift pattern)
C6OZ-6392-C	1968–1970 manual transmissions. Beginning on February 15, 1968, the C6OZ-6392-C casting number was changed to C6OA-6394-D. The C60A-6394-D number is correct for 390-4V after February 15, 1968, and all 1968–1970 428 Cobra Jets.
C6OR-7A040-D	1966/1968 Comet/Fairlane 427/428, 1967 Cobra 427, and 1967/1968 Mustang GT500 428; Machined for center pattern, 31 spline
C7OR-7A040-A	1967/1969 Comet/Fairlane/Falcon and 1967/1969 Cougar/Mustang 390-4V; Machined for 28 spline
C7OR-7A040-A	1968/1969 Mustang/Cougar 428; Machined for 31 spline
RF-C8AR-7A040-B	1968–1969 LTD, Galaxie, Custom 390; 17-inch length; 28 spline
C8AR-7A040-B	1968 Galaxie/Monterey 428
C8AR-7A040-C	1968 Galaxie/Monterey (excluding the 428)
RF-C9AR-7A040A	1969 Galaxie Custom 429; 17-inch length; 31 spline
C9OR-7A040-A	1969 Comet/Fairlane/Monterey 428/429-4V and 1969 Comet/Fairlane 351/390 with 31 spline
C9AR-7A040-A	1969 Galaxie 429
C9OR-7A040-A	1969-and-up Cyclone/Torino/Ranchero 302, 428, and 429; 17-inch length; 31 spline
DOZR-7A040-A	Three front shifter mounting holes drilled and tapped. Same as shifter location as C6O and C7O; 14-inch length; 28 spline
DOZR-7A040-A	Three rear shifter mounting holes drilled and tapped; 1970–1971 Cougar/Mustang 428, 429, and Boss 429; 14-inch length; 31 spline
DKT (David Kee Toploaders)	1964–1965 Falcon, 1964–1973 Cougar/Mustang, 1966–1968 Cyclone/Fairlane/Ranchero/Torino 289 302, and 390; 1966–1969 Falcon 289 and 302; 1966–1969 Cougar/Mustang 390; 1967-and-up Cyclone/Fairlane 427 and 428; 1968–1969 Mustang 428 and 429; 14-inch length; 28 or 31 spline

This factory tailhousing shows the casting numbers at the rear of the piece. The simple three-bolt-mounting design for the shifter and/or its mounting plate is also shown. Much like the tailhousing itself, the holes for the shifter came in various designs.

Ford used two patterns on the back of its small-block engines for bolting it to the bellhousing. The back of this Ford engine block shows the five-bolt pattern along with the two mounting/locating pins (one on each side) for lining up the bellhousing.

C4DR-7A040-A is a Comet/Falcon extension tailhousing. This casting had provisions for either the forward Comet/Falcon shifter mounting or the rear Mustang shifter mounting. If the casting was machined for the Comet/Falcon pattern, the Mustang rear bosses were not machined. If the casting was machined for the Mustang, the Falcon pattern lower two bosses were machined flat. The upper Comet/Falcon boss was either left as a cast boss or machined flat with the other two bosses. Later service replacements had the upper boss completely machined off.

C4ZR-7A040-A is a Mustang extension housing that did not have a pattern for the Comet or Falcon. The Mustang used both housings (appropriately machined).

C6OR-7A040-C was machined as necessary for the center pattern (intermediates) or the rear pattern (Mustang). It was only used with 28-spline output shafts.

C6OR-7A040-D was similar to the previously mentioned housing extensions but was made for 31-spline output shafts. It has both patterns, but only the center pattern is machined. There were no Mustangs in 1966 with 31-spline output shafts, so the rear pattern was never machined.

C7OR-7A040-A could be machined for the center or rear pattern and a 28- or 31-spline output shaft.

Bellhousing Codes

Ford created 19 different bellhousings to fit numerous engine/transmission and car/truck amalgamations. The 385-series big-block engines have a different bellhousing bolt pattern than the FE-series big-block engines. They also used two different bolt patterns on the back of the engine where the bellhousing would bolt up. The 1964-and-newer small-block engines had five bolts for the bellhousing. The five-bolt bellhousing uses the smaller 4 11/16-inch outside-diameter bearing retainer. The six-bolt bellhousing uses the larger 4⅞-inch outside-diameter bearing retainer, and it was used on 1965-and-newer big-block engines.

A quick way to check the fitment for a Toploader is to measure the overall depth of the bellhousing to determine how the depth of the bellhousing will match/fit the input shaft. Place the bellhousing on a flat surface with the larger opening facing down. Measure straight down into the hole in the center from the flat surface to across the top of the bellhousing. If a bellhousing has a depth of 6¼ inches, it is for a Toploader. If the bellhousing is a 1/2 inch deeper (6¾ inches), it is a truck bellhousing and will not work.

All of the small-block engine bellhousings fit up to 1973. Bellhousings for big-blocks can cause problems, and FE engines should be checked carefully because they were also used in Ford's truck lines.

The casting numbers on a bellhousing can be found inside and outside of the bellhousing.

Bellhousing Casting Numbers		
Casting Number(s)	**Year(s)**	**Engine(s)**
C3AA-6394-C	1963–1964	289
C3AA-6394-A	1963–1964	390, 406, and 427
C3AA-6394-C	1965	289, 5-bolt block
C5DA-6394-A	1965–1967	289, 6-bolt block
C5AA-6394-A	1965–1967	390, 427, and 428 (11-inch clutch)
C5AA-6394-B	1969–1973	302
C5TA-6394-A	1969–1970	351
C6OA-6394-B and D	1969	390 GT; 11½-inch clutch. Beginning on February 15, 1968, the C6OZ-6392-C casting number was changed to C6OA-6394-D. The C60A-6394-D number is correct for the 390-4V after February 15, 1968, and all of 1968–1970 428 Cobra Jets.
C6OA-6394-B and D	1969	428 CJ-SCJ
C6OZ-6392-C	1968/1970	428 CJ-SCJ; includes 3-speeds (390 only) and 4-speeds
C6OZ-6392-C	1970	428 CJ-SCJ. Some research indicates that beginning on February 15, 1968, the casting number was changed to C6OA-6394-D. For originality, the C60A-6394-D number is correct for the 390-4V after February 15, 1968, and all 1968–1970 428 Cobra Jets.
C8AA-6394-A (Aluminum)	1968	289, 302
C8AA-6394-B (Cast Iron)	1968–1969	302
C8OA-6394-A	1968–1969	390 GT, 428 CJ; 11-1/2-inch clutch
C80A-6394-A	1968–1969	428 CJ-SCJ (after February 15, 1968)
C9AA-6394-C	1969	390, 428; 11-inch clutch
C9AA-6394-D	1969–1970	429
C9AA-6394-E	1970–1971	429 Boss (after February 2, 1970)
D1TE-6394-AA	1971	351
D1TA-6394-AA	1972–1973	351

These two Ford bellhousings show the difference between the five- and six-hole patterns for mounting the bellhousings. The bellhousing on the left is for early Toploaders, which is evidenced by the smaller bolt pattern for bolting the transmission case to the bellhousing.

Casting Date Codes

Casting date codes require patience because they are cast into cast iron and can be difficult to read or may be unreadable. Also, these codes were made by screwing tags into the granular molds, and molds often literally fell apart in those areas. In addition, the formats used for coding them were not always consistent.

Casting date codes are located after the casting number on the case and tailhousing. The molds had a small changeable plate that was held in place by a screw at each end. You can actually see the casting reflection of the plate with the screws fastening it to the mold on some pieces.

Date codes are usually a letter followed by numbers. The first letter is the month. The letter "I" was not used, so that it would not be confused with the number "1."

Date Code	Month
A	January
B	February
C	March
D	April
E	May
F	June
G	July
H	August
J	September
K	October
L	November
M	December

A typical casting code is shown on the driver's side of this Toploader. Below is the detent bolt for third/fourth gear and two of the three cams and shafts that attach to the shifter's rods. Note the bottom line of the casting number and the section on the right that clearly show the screwdriver imprint.

Another transmission's example of a date code is shown here. This one, which is also on the driver's side, has its numbers in a different location. Again, the straight-slot screwdriver imprint is visible at the end of the date code. The transmission's silver paint makes it easier to read.

The next character (or two characters) is the day of the month: 1 through 31.

If there are three numbers, the last number is the year.

- 4-64
- 5-65
- 6-66
- 7-67
- 8-68
- 9-69
- 0-70
- 1-71
- 2-72
- 3-73

Examples:

- C4AR main cases were used in 1964 only, so they only have the month and day that they were cast.
- C5AR main cases were used from 1965 to 1967. If it has a date code of A127, it was cast on January 12, 1967.
- C8AR main cases were used from 1968 to 1971. If it has a date code of M99, it was cast on December 9, 1969.
- D2AR main cases were used from late 1971 to 1972. If it has a date code of J52, it was cast on September 5, 1972.

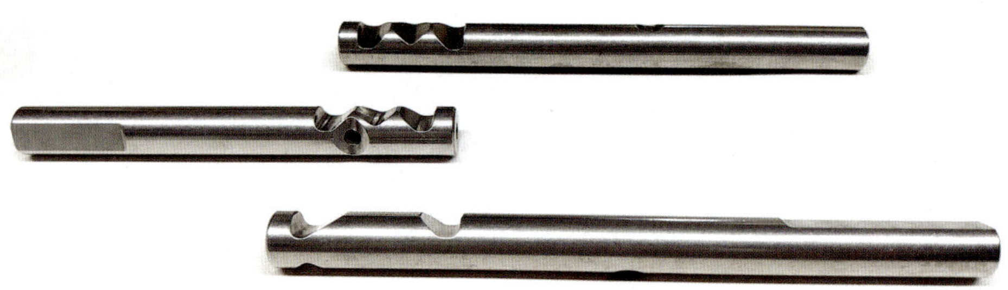

Three different shift rails were used in Toploaders. They vary by the years they were used and differ in their location. Keep them separate along with their detents and springs because they need to match up. Otherwise, they will not work correctly. (Photo Courtesy David Randal)

Shift-Rail Identification

Shift rails for Toploaders come in sets of three. There were six different applications created over the various production runs of the Toploader. They are not interchangeable within the transmission and should be kept separate and labeled for position any time they are removed. The shift rails are categorized by year and type in the following table. The descriptions help to differentiate them.

Application Year(s)	Type and Description
Early 1964–1965	Type 1: two hatchet-head and three round detents; one interlock pin; three short, heavy springs
1966–1967	Type 2: five blunt-point detents; one interlock pin; three heavy, short springs
1968–1969	Type 3: five sharp-point detents; one interlock pin; two short, heavy springs; one long, heavy spring
1969	Type 4: five blunt-point detents; one interlock pin; two short, heavy springs; one long, heavy spring
1970	Type 5: five black pointed detents; one interlock pin; two short, heavy springs; one long, heavy spring
Part of 1971, all of 1972–1973	Type 6: five black pointed detents; one tall detent; two interlock pins; three short, heavy springs; one short, light spring. Used in D2 casting number cases.

Additional detent identification can be found in their lengths. There are five types of heads with only three lengths. If the detents are not modified, worn, or damaged, they should be the following lengths:

Head Type and Length	
Type	**Length**
Round head	0.393 inch
Hatchet head	0.393 inch
Short point	0.427 inch
Blunt point	0.427 inch
Long point	0.459 inch

Gear Ratios

Toploader gear ratios were made in two styles: wide ratio and close ratio. Ratio identification from the outside of the transmission can only be made with correct tag numbers and letters. Again, there should be some skepticism when relying on the tag solely for identification. Read the warning at the beginning of this chapter for more information about ascertaining the correct information.

Wide- and close-ratio Toploaders have different cluster or counter gears. While it's obvious that the first through third gears inside of a Toploader need dedicated gears for each model, many people forget that the

These two new gears are close-ratio, third-gear units for a Toploader. The gear on the left has packing coating on it. Note the cones that merge with the synchronizers, the engagement gears that mesh with the blocker rings, and the lubrication holes that keep everything well oiled. The darker gear on the right has been coated with a dry-lube finish. (Photo Courtesy David Randal)

Wide- and close-ratio gears are often difficult to differentiate. The bottom input shaft is a wide-ratio unit, and the top input shaft is a close-ratio unit. The output shaft between them is a 31-spline model. (Photo Courtesy David Randal)

cluster gear must also have the necessary matching gears to transmit power to the output shaft. Therefore, any listing of which gear has which ratio needs to include the cluster gear and its corresponding tooth count. This means that the cluster gear needs to match the ratios. This must be factored in when buying separate new gears or complete gearsets. When ordering a new gearset, there are two styles of cluster gears from which to choose: wide ratio and close ratio.

This is a closer look at the second gear of a close-ratio Toploader. It has 28 gear teeth, and the engagement teeth are seen in a smaller circle on the side of the gear. The engagement teeth mesh with the blocker ring to make the connection with the synchronizer.

Note how the count of cluster-gear teeth vary between wide- and close-ratio versions.

There is a quick and easy way to identify a Toploader gear ratio. Remove the cover and count the teeth on the second gear. Counting from the rear of the transmission, the second gear is the second one on the output shaft. It is next to the first/second-gear synchronizer and then first gear, which is the rearmost gear on the output shaft. Do not count the straight-cut teeth on the outside of the first/second-gear synchronizer

Close-Ratio Toploaders				
Gear	First	Second	Third	Fourth
Ratio	2.32	1.69	1.29	1.0
Tooth Count	32	28	25	23
Cluster Gear Tooth Count	15	18	21	25

Wide-Ratio Toploaders				
Gear	First	Second	Third	Fourth
Ratio	2.78	1.93	1.36	1.0
Tooth Count	32	31	25	23
Cluster Gear Tooth Count	15	21	24	30

Cluster gears are one-piece gears with four different gears machined onto them. They come in two versions (wide ratio and close ratio) and need to match the ratio of the forward gears. Note the oil holes and the two raised rings on the bottom version. The rings indicate wide-ratio gears, and all cluster shafts have oiling holes (the cluster shaft's oiling holes in the top version are not visible in this photo.)

The subtle differences can be seen by placing the two input shafts next to each other. The bigger one (right) shows the shaft thickness, and the smaller one shows the length of pilot shafts. (Photo Courtesy David Kee)

because that is used for the reverse gear. If second gear has 31 teeth, it is a wide-ratio unit. If it has 28 teeth, it is a close-ratio model.

No Serial Numbers

There are generally no complete serial numbers on Toploader cases, tailhousings, or any other external component. The same is true for all internal parts. The only known exception is a partial vehicle identification number (VIN) stamped into Toploader cases on the driver-side upper ear on production high-performance Ford cars. These are usually found on Boss, Cobra Jet, Super Cobra Jet, Mach 1, and other high-performance models. In addition, some of the early K-Code Mustang Toploaders have stampings on the bottom center of the case that show the complete VIN.

No Codes on Input Shafts

Ford did not put any codes on Toploader input shafts. That would have helped when trying to differentiate them from each other. Knowing the differences can help avoid mistakes because the differences are small and hard to see. For example, running a short shaft behind a small-block engine would result in poor shifting, jumping out of gear, and, ultimately, front bearing failure.

Measuring the input shaft reveals which one is which. The diameter of the input shaft is critical. There are two sizes, and they were used in both wide- or close-ratio models. The smaller one is 1 1/16 inches in diameter, and the larger one is 1 3/8 inches in diameter.

The 1 3/8-inch input shafts were only available in close-ratio units from the factory and had the shorter 3/4-inch length pilot bushing surface. The 1 1/16-inch input shaft was available in wide- and close-ratio units in small-block and big-block (390) applications. In many descriptions of Toploaders, the words "big in" or "little in" are used, and this refers to the input-shaft size. "Big out" or "little out" refers to the output-shaft size.

As far as the length of pilot bushing surfaces, Ford big-blocks require a 3/4-inch-length pilot bushing surface. Small-blocks require a 1¼-inch-length pilot bushing surface. The pilot bushing diameter is the same size on both.

Input-Shaft Conversions

Input-shaft conversions are possible because one-piece input shafts can be swapped. A 1 3/8-inch input shaft can be installed into a 1 1/16-inch Toploader to convert it to a large-input unit. ■

CHAPTER 3

How Toploaders Work

Muscle car–era manual transmissions typically work solely through mechanical actions. They begin with an engaged clutch that turns the transmission's input shaft. From there, internal interchanging gears are mechanically shifted as desired. The chosen geared power is delivered (mostly via a cluster gear, sometimes called a secondary gear shaft) to the transmission's output shaft.

Then, the splined connections of the output shaft and the vehicle's driveshaft connect to turn the rear differential and its wheels. There is no hydraulic programming like there is in an automatic transmission, and every change is a mechanical movement that needs to be manually initiated by the driver using the clutch and shifter.

Toploaders use these principles but offer efficiency and speed improvements over the other brands. One of the biggest improvements in the Toploader is its use of synchronizer-sleeve gears moved by shift forks instead of traditional sliding gears to accomplish gear changes.

First, second, and third gear on a Toploader ride on the output shaft and do not change their positions. The synchronizers move between the gears and allow for faster shifts, as the gears mesh smoother and quicker. Because of this more-efficient meshing, synchronizers also reduce gear impact when the gears meet, and that can reduce subsequent component wear.

The sliding gears that are used in other transmissions can also take longer to fully engage. Because they basically mesh under varying degrees of impact, they can also wear quicker than the Toploader's synchronizer system. These traits quickly became favorable for motorsports and performance use, and they made the Toploader very popular in those areas.

Faster shifts provide an obvious advantage in drag racing. For oval-track and road racing, the faster shifts that also came with the synchronizer sleeve system allowed for upshifts or downshifts to any forward gear while in motion. These traits make the Toploader a very popular 4-speed even today. In fact, many modern day 4-speeds have incorporated selected Toploader aspects.

Inside a Toploader are three gear shafts. Two of the three shafts are used for forward movement, and the third is used for reverse movement. Both forward gear shafts are in constant rotation anytime the clutch

Two Toploader gear shafts are shown. The top gear shaft is the one-piece cluster gear. Below the cluster gear is the reverse idler-gear shaft. On the bottom is the reverse shift rail and its fork.

When the cover is removed from a Toploader, this is what it looks like. In this case, the two shift forks (items 5 and 14) have been upgraded to stronger aftermarket high-performance pieces. Outside of that, the parts in this Toploader are stock and are in their stock locations. Note the relationship to the gears on the output shaft and how the synchronizers are located between the pairs of gears that they engage on that shaft. In addition, note the axis of the shift rails to the output shaft. They are parallel, and that contributes to smoother shift-fork and synchronizer arc-swing movements. Other pieces and assemblies inside the case are not visible in this photo. They are detailed elsewhere in this book. (Photo Courtesy David Kee)

1. *Case (the front of the case that bolts to the bellhousing)*
2. *Input shaft*
3. *Input-shaft engagement teeth*
4. *Fourth-gear blocker ring*
5. *Third/fourth-gear shifter fork (aftermarket version)*
6. *Third/fourth-gear synchronizer*
7. *Third-gear blocker ring*
8. *Third-gear engagement teeth*
9. *Third gear*
10. *Second gear*
11. *Second-gear engagement teeth*
12. *Second-gear blocker ring*
13. *First/second-gear synchronizer (with straight-cut gears used for reverse on circumference)*
14. *First/second-gear shift fork (aftermarket version)*
15. *First-gear blocker ring*
16. *First-gear engagement teeth*
17. *First gear*
18. *Output-shaft bearing*
19. *Case (the back of the case where the tailhousing bolts up)*
20. *Third/fourth shift rail*
21. *Hole for detent and spring for first/second gear*
22. *Shift rail for reverse*
23. *Shift rail for first/second*
24. *Shift-fork set screws (2)*

This single shaft is the output shaft. Gears that ride on the output shaft mesh with the cluster gear and turn other gears (and eventually turn the driveshaft). The output shaft is also connected to the reverse gear when those two are engaged.

Gear-Shaft Basics for Transmissions

Gear shafts can act as an axle within a transmission system. They create rotation that allows one gear to transmit its power/force and rotate single or multiple gears. Similar to gears and gear shafts in a transmission, they help transfer horsepower from the engine to the driving wheels. This process also turns horsepower into torque to power those wheels. Gear styles can use straight-tooth, beveled, spiral, or helical gears.

Gear shafts can be shafts that have gears machined directly into them, and there are a few absolute truths regarding them. The first is that when gear shafts are properly installed, the gears have no lateral movement along their shafts. More accurately, the shafts and gears are fixed into their position and do not move from that position. They are only there to provide a place for the gears to axis and transmit motion and energy.

A second absolute truth is that when gear shafts are correctly locked into their position with no lateral movement, the gears are kept in proper alignment. This allows them to do their job with the best-possible mesh and least-possible slop (poor mesh and slop results in a loss of power). It also keeps the gears in tolerance alignment, so that the gear mesh is neither too tight nor too loose, causing too much or not enough working friction. Too much friction can cause drag, reducing efficiency.

When the gears are fixed to a shaft and are engaged or disengaged, it's the synchronizer that moves laterally, not the shaft or gears. Gear shafts can also be the type that are comprised of separate components and need to have every component in alignment to work efficiently. ■

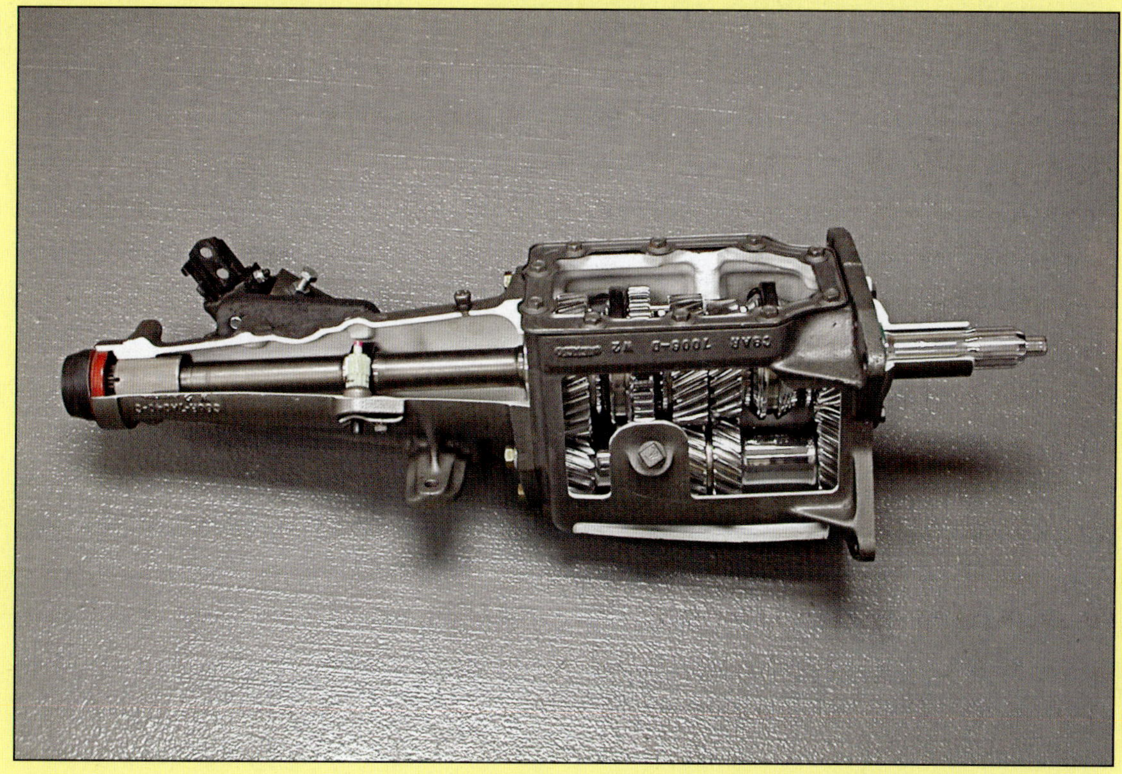

This Toploader cutaway by David Kee shows its overall simplicity. Note the plane of the input and output shafts and how they align and interact with the clutch and driveshaft. In addition, note the cluster gear that is riding slightly below that plane but is still engaging that primary shaft line. (Photo Courtesy David Randal)

is engaged, and motion is sent into the transmission, even in neutral when the output shaft's gears are not engaged.

The Toploader transmission's input and output shafts run along the centerline of the case and are on the same plane as the engine's crankshaft and the car's driveshaft at the end of the tailhousing. The input shaft, located at the front of the case, has the shorter length of the two. The output shaft, the longer shaft, includes all forward gears. The two shafts engage when certain gear combinations are selected by the driver via the shifter, and they disengage the same way for other gear combinations.

The other forward gear shaft, a one-piece cluster gear with its four gears, is located slightly under and to the outside of the output shaft. The cluster gear is also known as a counter or secondary gear. It acts as an idler, completing the engagement of the first, second, and third gears that are located on the output or main shaft as well as engaging the reverse idler when needed.

While it is not considered one of the Toploader's gear shafts, the input shaft includes a large, external gear. That gear engages the cluster gear to give it constant motion. The small engagement teeth seen next to the bigger gear engage the third/fourth-gear synchronizer when fourth gear is engaged.

Toploader gear shafts interact with each other like this: From the top is the reverse-gear shaft, the cluster-gear shaft, the input shaft (left), and the output shaft (right) with all of the gears on it. Note the relationship to the gears' meshing. The gear teeth on the bottom row, left side are the gears on the input shaft. They mesh with the gears above them on the cluster gear. Note the types of gears on the reverse shaft and how they mesh. The straight-cut gears mesh with the straight-cut gear on the outside of the first/second-gear synchronizer for reverse motion. (Photo Courtesy David Randal)

The last of the three gear shafts is the reverse idler shaft, which has its own gears that come into play only when reverse is activated. Reverse also gets its power from the cluster gear. Shifting into reverse engages the reverse-gear shaft with the first/second-gear synchronizer's external gear to transmit reverse directional power to the output shaft and driveshaft. Basically, the simple addition of one more gear is what causes the direction to reverse.

Shifting

The shifting sequence begins when the driver engages the clutch and moves the shifter to the desired gear position. The shifter's linkage rotates a cam lever on a shaft on the outside of the driver's side of the main case. Positioning that shaft rotates another cam lever on the shaft's other end inside the transmission. This cam lever then moves the associated shift fork that engages or disengages its synchronizer, selecting or deselecting the chosen gear.

Shift rails provide the anchors for the pivot points of the shift forks and incorporate a more solid and better geometric base point between the moving parts for more precision and effectiveness. Shift rails are located inside the case on the driver's side (where the shifter cam levers come into the case). The cam and lever move the fork, which is locked to the shift

Helical, Angled, and Straight-Cut Gears

All forward gears in a Toploader are helical or angled, but the reverse gears are straight cut. The reverse sliding gear on the exterior of the first/second-speed synchronizer is also a straight-cut gear so that it will mesh with the reverse gear when it is engaged. Inside, the synchronizers are spur-style gears to provide better mesh during gear changes.

Toploaders used several styles of gears. Gears are used for input and output shafts, internal and external couplings, synchronizers, and transmitting motion as in the cluster gear, energy, and torque. Straight-cut gears are exclusively used for reverse-gear functions.

Two examples of gears in a Toploader are shown. The gear on the left is a helical gear—in this case, second gear. The gear on the right is a straight-cut gear on the outside of the first/second-gear synchronizer, which affects the reverse gear to the driveshaft when it is engaged.

The gear teeth are more visible from the ends of the gear shafts. From left to right are the reverse-gear idler, the input shaft, and the cluster gear. Only the reverse-gear idler has straight-cut teeth on it. Note that needle bearings are installed in all of the gears. (Photo Courtesy David Randal)

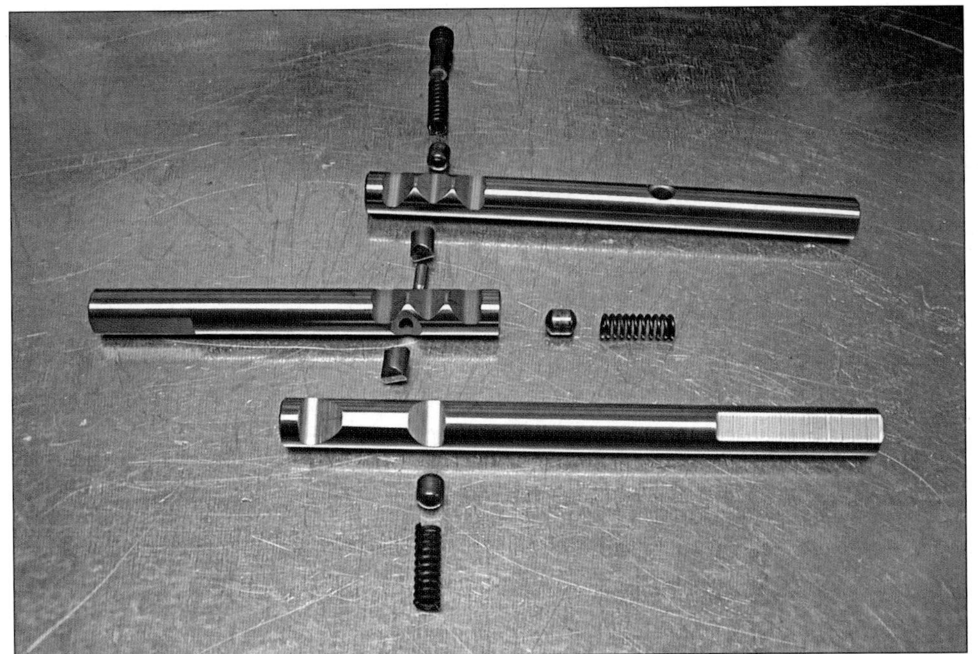

This display of three shift rails and their detents, springs, and plugs not only shows the number that is used but also how they interact with each other. Their main job is to prevent two or more gears from shifting at the same time by locking out those that the driver does not want to shift. (Photo Courtesy David Randal)

The shift rails in their positions inside the transmission show how they relate to the detents and detent holes in the case. In this view, the driver's side of the case is acting as the back wall to the shift rails. (Photo Courtesy David Randal)

This Toploader case cutaway shows how shift rails interact with each other and the detents that keep them in orientation to prevent the transmission from shifting into more than one gear at a time. The part of the case that tunnels the detents has been cut away to show how they align to work with all three shift rails. Note how they interact with the cam and shift levers that control their movements. (Photo Courtesy David Kee)

rail by its set screw. The shift rail keeps the shift fork in its alignment, parallel to the output shaft. That makes for a more matching movement of the fork and output shaft compared to other OEM 4-speeds that had forks using more of an arc for their travel.

Toploader shift rails come in matching sets of three, and they rest in bosses that have been cast into the main case. The shift rails are designed and work where only one gear can be engaged at a time, thus avoiding the catastrophic result of engaging two gears at once. This is accomplished with detents and matching detent seats on the shift rails. Once engaged, the selected gear then engages the output shaft to turn the driveshaft.

When shifting gears, the dynamics of the Toploader act as other manual transmissions do: advancing a gear takes it out of any other gear that it may already be in. When the driver shifts to a new gear, the appropriate shifter rod moves that shifter arm in the correct direction to disengage the previous gear or take it out of neutral. The shifter rods essentially transmit the dedicated functions of engaging or disengaging a gear when selected by the cam levers and their shafts. All forward gear shifts, up or down, are made in a like manner because the gear shafts are in constant mesh.

Cam levers are moved by shifter rods on the outside of a case, and they move shift forks inside the box. The flat part (seen here on the left) acts as a cam to move the shift fork inside the case. The long, round shaft goes through the hole in the case with the threaded shaft for the nuts holding on the shift lever. Note the O-ring that prevents any leakage.

On a Toploader, there are three such cam levers and shafts on the outside of the driver's side of the case. Two are for forward gears and one is for reverse. Of the two engaging forward gears, the rearward one is for first and second and the one nearest the front of the transmission is for third and fourth. This matches the inside locations of the synchronizers on the output shaft of the transmission. The reverse cam and its shaft are the one in the middle of the three. In addition, the two forward-gear cam levers and shafts operate like three-position switches with one gear as neutral and the other gear in its range of motion. Reverse gear is more like a light switch in that it's either on or off (in gear or out of gear).

Gears

When the driver engages first gear, the shifter rods move the first/second shifter cam lever, which moves the first/second-gear shift fork on its shift rail. (See the photo at the beginning of this chapter for reference.) The first/second-gear shift fork is the rearward-located one, and it engages the first/second-gear synchronizer sleeve, moving it toward the rear of the transmission and first gear.

When this movement and pressure is applied to the blocker ring, it acts as a cone clutch to match the speed of the gear with the speed of the output shaft. This action provides smooth, synchronized shifts up or down. When shifting into first gear from idle and the vehicle is not moving, the output shaft is not turning, so the blocker ring stops any rotation of the gearset after the clutch is pushed in.

Full engagement of the outer hub with first gear locks the first/second-gear synchronizer assembly to first gear via its internal splines. The synchronizer assemblies are positively connected to the output shaft by internal splines. When one of the outer hubs is moved toward the gear being selected, the blocker ring matches the gear speed and the output-shaft speed to perform a smooth shift with no grinding.

First

Shifting into first simultaneously couples the cluster gear to fully engage first gear. At this point, the input shaft is disengaged from the output shaft. Both are rotating in the same direction at different RPM because the ratio selected runs through the cluster gear.

The input shaft and output shaft always rotate independently in every gear except fourth. The cluster gear is in constant mesh so that action is always complete. Once the shift has been accomplished, the circuit of gears from first gear down to the corresponding gear on the cluster gear and back up to the input shaft is complete. When fully engaged, this "circuit" of gears is complete and now turns the output shaft, which turns the driveshaft.

Second

When shifting from first to second gear, several things happen at once. The shift rods move the first/second shifter cam lever in the opposite direction to disengage first gear. In addition, the shift fork moves from first gear to neutral to second gear, moving the first/second-gear synchronizer forward out of first gear, into neutral, and then into second gear.

Second gear is mounted forward of first gear on the output shaft and on the forward side of the first/second-gear synchronizer. As with first gear, the cluster gear is now engaged to complete the second-gear connection of motion to the output shaft going onto the driveshaft. Also like first gear, the input and output shafts are not engaged directly with each other and are rotating independently.

Third

Shifting into third gear fully disconnects the first/second-gear synchronizer and second gear and returns them to neutral. The third/fourth-gear shift cam lever is now actuated and moves the third/fourth-gear shift fork and its synchronizer, which is located toward the front of the output shaft. The synchronizer is then moved rearward to engage third gear with the cluster gear. This engages the output shaft and then the driveshaft. When third gear is engaged, the input and output shafts are still disengaged from each other.

Fourth

There are two trains of thought regarding what comprises fourth gear in a Toploader. Some folks think that the gear on the inside end of the input shaft is fourth gear. Others believe that there is no actual fourth gear. The bottom line is that the output shaft and driveshaft operate at a 1:1 ratio when they are locked up with the input shaft.

So, how does that happen? When fourth gear is chosen, the third/fourth-gear synchronizer sleeve moves away from third gear, passes through neutral toward the input shaft, and locks that in place with the output shaft. This movement connects the outer sleeve of the third/fourth-gear synchronizer with the engagement teeth on the inside end of the input shaft. Locking the input and output shafts together allows engine power to directly transmit straight to the driveshaft with a 1:1 ratio.

So, the big gear on the input shaft does not actually turn the output shaft. That big gear engages the cluster gear to keep it in the constant rotation that was mentioned in the first-gear description. The only time that the two shafts are directly engaged is when the transmission is in fourth gear. With no actual gear transmitting fourth-gear power, there truly is no fourth gear on the gearset of the output shaft, as it and the input-shaft coupling make that connection with both shafts directly feeding the driveshaft.

Reverse

Shifting into reverse begins with all forward gears being in neutral and the input shaft and the output shaft not being connected. The reverse shift fork moves the reverse-gear shaft into play. One of the two gears on the reverse-gear counter shaft has helical gears cut into it, and it engages with the cluster gear that turns the reverse-gear shaft. The other reverse gear, with straight-cut teeth, matches with the straight-cut gear on the outside of the first/second-gear synchronizer. When the two meet, that transmits reverse rotational power to the output shaft and then the driveshaft. The first/second-gear synchronizer is the only one with this type of external gear with straight-cut teeth in a Toploader.

Those noticing how reverse is such a low gear can understand that it is basically the same ratio as first gear but rotates in the opposite direction. However, as the straight-cut gear on the outside of the first/second-gear synchronizer does not mesh with any other gear until it's shifted into reverse, it affects nothing. It's just going along for the ride until it is needed.

It's evident there is a lot going on inside a Toploader transmission when shifting through the gears. So, a Toploader's components need to be in proper alignment and in good working order to get great results. A careful disassembly and thorough inspection are the first steps to make sure that all of the parts are in good working order during a rebuild.

The bigger gear on an input shaft is not fourth gear. Instead, it engages with the cluster gear to keep it turning when the input shaft is rotating. The smaller engagement teeth next to the gear connect with the outer sleeve of the third/fourth gear synchronizer to form the connection that is fourth gear.

DISASSEMBLY

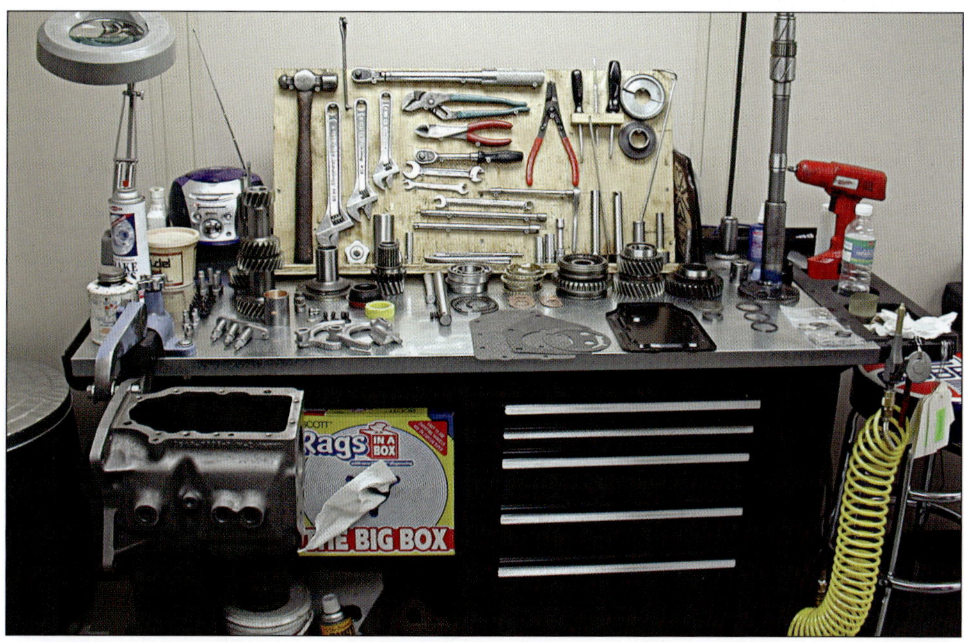

An important part of working on the disassembly and reassembly of an item such as a transmission is creating and maintaining a workspace. This clean and well-lit workspace was organized by David Kee. Everything from rags to compressed air is easily accessible. (Photo Courtesy David Randal)

Details that you learn during the disassembly of complicated parts will help during assembly. The goal for this chapter is to create a comprehensive, step-by-step list for disassembling a Toploader. In addition, working backward in the assembly sequence can also help a new builder learn about the parts and their locations and understand how they fit and work together. The following table shows the tools that are needed for disassembly and assembly.

During disassembly, keep the parts organized. Although it adds another step to the process, it makes

This Toploader is in a device that was specially made for the job. The main benefit of using this device is to allow access at every angle necessary for reassembly. (Photo Courtesy David Randal)

The Toploader is bolted to the holding fixture with two bolts on the passenger's side of the transmission. This allows work to be done with the Toploader in either the horizontal or vertical position. Between the holding fixture and the workbench, the 100-plus-pound transmission requires a stable platform. (Photo Courtesy David Randal)

retrieving a part much easier. It is inefficient to look for a part that you need in an unorganized pile of parts.

Gasket removal is optional during disassembly because most builders do this during a dedicated cleaning operation before beginning the inspection process. Don't throw away any parts—even parts that are already planned for replacement. Rebuild kits vary in what they include as well as the fitment of those parts, and no one wants to be missing a part and have to halt the assembly process to order a part. Most importantly, old parts can be used for comparison with new parts during

Tools for Disassembly and Assembly	
Supplies	• Clean, lint-free rags • Brake-parts cleaner or mineral spirits • Permatex Ultra Grey sealer • 80-grit emery cloth and 320-grit sandpaper • Purple medium-strength Scotch-Brite pad • Purple medium-strength, 3-inch Scotch-Brite surface-preparation discs for air tool use
Sockets, Wrenches, and Ratchets	• 3/8-inch-drive and 1/4-inch-drive ratchets • 6-inch 1/4-inch-drive extension • 3-inch 3/8-inch-drive extension • 12-inch 3/8-inch-drive socket • 3/8-inch-drive torque wrench (15- to 50-ft-lb range) • 1/2-inch 6-point 3/8-inch-drive deep socket • 9/16-inch 6-point 3/8-inch-drive deep socket • 5/8-inch 6-point 3/8-inch-drive shallow socket • 3/4-inch 6-point 3/8-inch-drive shallow socket • 5/32-inch Allen-head 1/4-inch-drive socket • 7/16-inch open-end wrench
Common Hand Tools	• 8-inch crescent (adjustable) wrench • Slip-joint pliers • Small, telescoping magnet • Square-tip, snap-ring pliers • Hammers • 1/2-inch-diameter brass punch • Phillips-head screwdriver • Flat-head screwdriver • Gasket scraper • Scribing tool with straight and 90-degree tips
Specialty Tools	• 90-degree 1/4-inch-drive air tool • Approximately 12-inch-long piece of 3/16-inch brake line with one end flared • Number 26–size bushing driver for 28 spline • Number 28–size bushing driver for 31 spline • Round piece of metal tubing that fits input- and output-shaft seals for even and correct installation

the inspection process, and this may reveal other related problems.

Rebuilding a Toploader is literally a one-step-at-a-time process and that includes disassembly. Let's begin with a Toploader that has been safely removed from the vehicle.

Having an unorganized pile of parts after disassembly can be a major problem when retrieving a part is required during reassembly. If a certain part, such as a roller bearing, is needed, finding the correct one would require measuring all of them to confirm that the correct part has been selected. It's more efficient to organize them one at a time during disassembly. (Photo Courtesy David Randal)

Disassembling a Toploader Transmission

1 *This amount of crud, dirt, and road grime is about average for a used Toploader. Don't be daunted by how the bulk of the grime is on the cover. (Photo Courtesy David Randal)*

2 *Some road grime has accumulated on this Toploader. Note that the threaded portions of the shifter cam and levers have nuts on them to protect the threads. (Photo Courtesy David Randal)*

3 *There is no easy way to drain all of the lubricant from a transmission without creating a mess. Toploaders have drain plugs, and a large pan can be used to keep the lubricant from becoming a mess on the bench.*

4 *Remove the 10 bolts from the Toploader's cover. Note the amount of resistance when unscrewing them to note any threads that may be stripped. Note where the two longer bolts were attached and any breaks in the cover gasket that would account for leaks.*

5 *After removing the cover, this Toploader looks good. All of the gears seem to have all their teeth, and everything seems to be in its proper place. However, a thorough inspection is needed.*

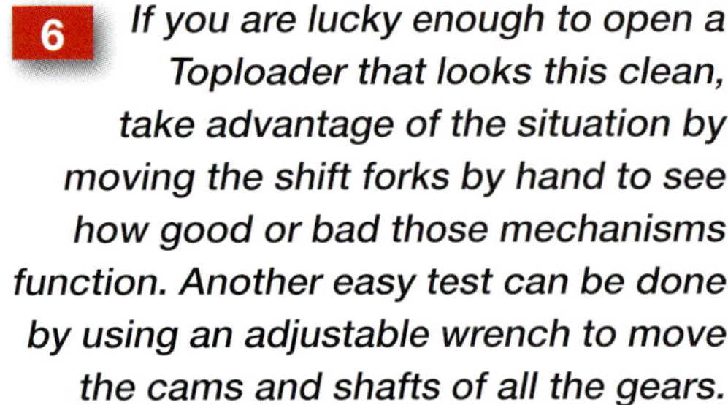

6 *If you are lucky enough to open a Toploader that looks this clean, take advantage of the situation by moving the shift forks by hand to see how good or bad those mechanisms function. Another easy test can be done by using an adjustable wrench to move the cams and shafts of all the gears.*

7 *This detailed photo (lower rail side) with the cover removed shows the straight-slot screw head holding one of the detents and its spring. Remove the screw and detent and organize them separately for their proper locations because Ford changed them over the years.*

8 *Remove the screw that holds the detent and its spring in place. Always keep detents, springs, and any of their fasteners separate because they are all not uniform in Toploaders. This removal may require a magnet. (Photo Courtesy David Randal)*

9 *Before removing the tailhousing seal, look for damage on and around the spline and seal. A damaged seal and/or end of the tailhousing may indicate additional damage inside on or around the output shaft and its spline.*

10 *This sequence shows how this specialized tool is used to remove the tailhousing bushing. First, the tool is positioned inside the seal with the lip of the tool passing completely through the inside diameter (ID) of the seal, where it will grab. (Photo Courtesy David Randal)*

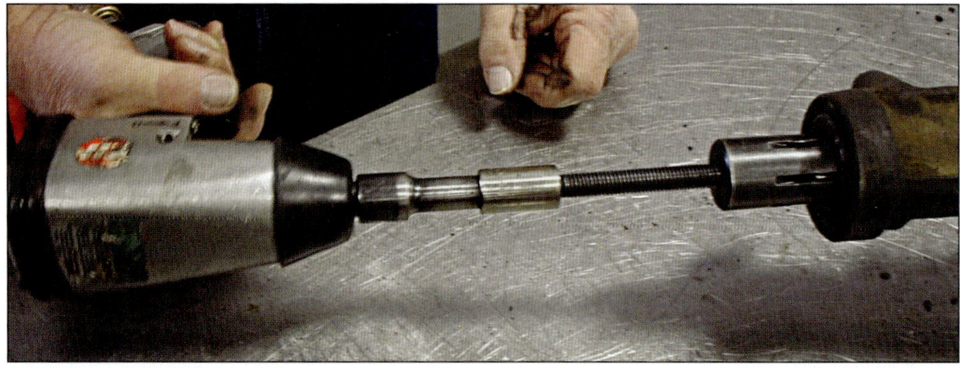

11 *Second, this specialized tool (a bushing puller) begins to expand inside the bushing as the shaft of the tool is turned. When it is fully expanded, the lip of the tool pulls the bushing straight and safely out of the tailhousing. (Photo Courtesy David Randal)*

12 *The tailhousing seal has been safely removed. Using a dedicated tool keeps collateral damage to a minimum. In this case, there is a bushing that can be easily damaged. In addition, the output shaft and the housing itself can be damaged. (Photo Courtesy David Randal)*

13 *Rear seals can be pried out if the appropriate removal tool is not available. The seal will likely be deformed and destroyed, but the important aspect is to not damage any contacting components. Be careful to not contact the output shaft, the tailhousing, the bushing, or nearby parts.*

14 *The tailhousing has five bolts that hold it onto the case. After they have been removed and the tailhousing has been broken free from the case, use two hands to pull the tailhousing straight off. Remember that the tailhousing is the piece that is being removed, not any of the internal components. The internal components stay with the case. (Photo Courtesy David Randal)*

15 *When the tailhousing is free of the case, pull it straight back, taking care to not damage the output shaft or the speedometer's components, such as the plastic gear. Those components stay connected to the output shaft, which is anchored in the case.*

16 *Finding a cut-off speedometer cable is good news for Toploader hunters. With the fitting still intact, it has likely protected the inside of the tailhousing from being contaminated by road debris, dirt, and grease. This may also have prevented the speedometer gear assembly from being damaged.*

17 *Toploaders used two ways to keep the speedometer gear correctly positioned on the output shaft: with a clip or with a snap ring. Either fastener needs to be removed for disassembly of the speedometer gear and its ball.*

18 When removing the snap ring for the speedometer gear, take care not to damage the plastic speedometer gear. Bracing the hand that is using the snap-ring pliers helps you maintain control of the tool and not allow it to slip. (Photo Courtesy David Randal)

19 The speedometer gear is plastic, so be careful when removing it if you intend to reuse it. It is rarely difficult to remove. However, if you have trouble removing it, use a long tool and small movements.

20 The ball for the speedometer gear is partially embedded into the output shaft. Removing it is easier with a magnet (as shown). The ball is the last of the three speedometer parts on the output shaft. (Photo Courtesy David Randal)

21 After removing the four 1/2-inch hex bolts that hold the input-shaft retainer on the front of the case, break the connection between the retainer and the case. A few hammer taps help if the retainer is stubborn due to being exposed to the elements, as it is an external component.

22 This is what the front input-shaft bearing looks like under the retainer. When first exposing it, watch for any broken pieces that may fall out if the bearing has been damaged. The bearing will be removed after the input shaft is removed.

23 Remove the tailhousing seal by using a prying action and a tool that will get under the old seal. This photo shows the seal being removed before the tailhousing has been removed from the case. It can also be removed later, during the cleaning stage.

24 Removing the cluster-gear shaft is essential to removing the input shaft. Drive the cluster-gear shaft out of the rear of the case with the aid of a socket extension and a hammer. Note how the line of the cluster-gear shaft is below the input- and output-shaft lines. (Photo Courtesy David Randal)

25 Remove the shaft for the cluster gear. Doing so accomplishes two things: 1) it begins the removal process for the internal parts and 2) it releases the engagement connection between the cluster gear and the input-shaft gears. This engagement needs to be broken to remove the input shaft.

26 *With the cluster-gear shaft removed from the rear of the case, the input shaft can be removed from the front of the case. The input-shaft bearing will also come out at this time because it is still attached to the input shaft.*

27 *After the input shaft has been removed from the case, it's not unusual for parts to come loose and even fall off the output shaft.*

28 *Looking from the back of the case, remove the set screw of the first/second-gear shift fork. This shift fork is the one next to the synchronizer that has straight-cut gears on it. (Photo Courtesy David Randal)*

29 *Hand pull the first/second-gear shift rail out of the case from the rail's hole in the rear face of the case. Using a similar-sized tool makes the alignment easier and reduces damage to both the rail and the case. (Photo Courtesy David Randal)*

30 *Sometimes, the shifter-mounting holes are covered with a shifter plate. This is usually on transmissions that have had aftermarket shifters installed. This Hurst shifter plate covers and uses the three holes in the tailhousing that held the factory shifter when the transmission was installed when the vehicle was first built.*

31 *Removing the snap ring for the rear main bearing allows you to remove the rear main bearing. Note the needle bearings in the hole for the cluster-gear shaft. It's not uncommon for the many needle bearings in a Toploader to come loose from their positions during disassembly.*

32 *Since the input shaft is shorter than the output shaft in length, the input shaft fits easily into a press to remove the front main bearing. Other methods (mentioned in the text of this book) that don't require the use of a press can be used. (Photo Courtesy David Randal)*

33 *Some builders use pry bars to remove the rear main bearing. A Toploader's rear main bearing is pressed onto the output shaft (not the main case). Avoid using pry bars because they will damage multiple output-shaft components.*

34 *Using a hammer and pry bar to drive the output shaft from the rear main bearing damages the rear main bearing, output shaft, first/second-gear synchronizer, and even the snap ring on the output shaft. Avoid using these methods and use a press.*

35 *Removing the third/fourth-gear shift fork and shift rail begins with the removal of its set screw (if it has not already been removed). This is the shift fork near the front of the case. Removing the actual shift fork requires some rotation and lifting at the same time to allow it to clear the synchronizer. (Photo Courtesy David Randal)*

36 *Lift the front of the output shaft by the third/fourth-gear synchronizer. The angle on the rear of the output shaft should be at the same angle. This allows the output shaft (with most of its components) to be lifted up and out of the case. Hold the thrust washer and first gear in place during this step. (Photo Courtesy David Randal)*

37 *With the output shaft removed, there is more working room to deal with the smaller assemblies. Remove the set screw for the reverse shift fork. This is the last shift-fork set screw to be removed. (Photo Courtesy David Randal)*

38 The reverse shift rail needs to be released from its detent and spring before it can be removed. Then, remove the reverse shift rail from the rear of the case. The detent and its spring can also be removed at this time. (Photo Courtesy David Randal)

39 With other components removed, there is ample clearance for the cluster gear to be removed from the case. The 42 needle bearings that seat inside the cluster gear may or may not still be in place at this time. Save them if they are to be reused. (Photo Courtesy David Randal)

40 Use a small tool to push the reverse-gear shaft out the rear of the case. Grabbing the reverse-gear shaft by the roll pin at the rear of the shaft may help you remove it. (Photo Courtesy David Randal)

41 With the reverse-gear shaft removed, the reverse idler gear can be removed from the case. This is the last of the gears and the last of the large pieces to be removed, so retrieval of smaller components, such as needle bearings, can take place now. (Photo Courtesy David Randal)

42 Remove all three cam levers. They include first/second, third/fourth, and reverse. They are shown with the reverse idler gear still in place, as this step can be done simultaneously. Note the needle bearing that has fallen into one of the reverse gears. (Photo Courtesy David Randal)

43 On a stable bench and from the front of the now-removed output shaft (or by the third/fourth-gear synchronizer), begin disassembling all of the output shaft's components by removing the most forward snap ring from the output shaft. (Photo Courtesy David Randal)

44 With the snap ring and thrust washer removed, the third/fourth-gear synchronizer can be removed from the output shaft. With a good grip, pull the synchronizer forward to remove it. Use a good working position with a flat surface. (Photo Courtesy David Randal)

45 Repeat this removal procedure for the bronze blocker ring and third gear. When removing these two pieces, note any excessive rocking of the components on the output shaft that may indicate worn pieces. A good grip on second gear can help. (Photo Courtesy David Randal)

46 *Remove the snap ring that holds second gear in place. Be careful to not "rack," or stretch, the snap ring. If you do, it will not be able to be reused. Open the snap ring just enough to gently slide it off the output shaft. (Photo Courtesy David Randal)*

47 *Remove the tanged thrust washer behind the snap ring. Take care not to scrape or nick the output shaft with the washer. The removal of this snap ring and tanged washer allows second gear to be removed. (Photo Courtesy David Randal)*

48 *Slide second gear off the output shaft, taking care not to scratch the surface, oil grooves, or splines of the output shaft. It may stick to the bronze blocker ring. Remember to hold the output shaft at a slight angle so that the gear will clear. (Photo Courtesy David Randal)*

49 *The blocker ring may separate from second gear, or it may stick to the first/second-gear synchronizer. The blocker ring must be removed as well. It may take some extra wiggling, as the blocker ring was engaged with second gear and the first/second-gear synchronizer. (Photo Courtesy David Randal)*

50 *After the blocker ring has been detached, the snap ring for the first/second-gear synchronizer is accessible and can be removed. Again, take care to save the snap ring and not damage the output shaft or other components. (Photo Courtesy David Randal)*

51 *Remove the first/second-gear synchronizer from the output shaft. Pulling the assembly straight and true to the front of the output shaft keeps damage to a minimum in nearby areas. Wiggling is required to clear the spline. (Photo Courtesy David Randal)*

52 *Now, the Toploader looks like nothing more than a collection of parts and a few assemblies. Keep the parts organized to increase efficiency during reassembly. (Photo Courtesy David Randal)*

Lubricant

Drain all of the lubricant from the unit. One way is to mount the transmission securely in position for gravity draining. If there is a drain plug, it is on the bottom of the case. From 1964 to mid-1970, drain plugs were on the bottom of the case. From late 1970 to 1973, drain plugs were not provided. The plug on the passenger's side of the case is the fill plug.

Cover, Pre-Cleaning, and Testing

Holding down a Toploader 4-speed's cover are 10 1/2-inch, serrated-flange, hex-head bolts. The bolts come in two lengths: eight 3/4-inch-long bolts and two 1-inch-long bolts. The 1-inch-long bolts go into the machined dowel holes on the driver-side front corner and passenger-side rear. Eight of the 10 holes are open holes, while the 2 on the bottom rear of the case are blind.

Remove the bolts, the cover, and as much of the gasket as possible from the case. The two bolt holes at the rear of the cover are blind. The bolt holes along the sides and at the front are open.

When the cover is removed, spray the inside with a cleaner and/or degreaser to further reduce the amount of gear oil inside. It will make inspection easier and will also begin the cleanup process.

To get an idea of how the transmission functions before disassembly, move the shift forks and synchronizers in and out of gear. If they move easily, it's likely that the builder will not find trouble in those areas. The same idea can be tried for moving the three cams and shafts of the gears with an adjustable wrench.

Detent Springs

Toploader detents are all different and they are location-specific on some models, so keep the location of all detents, their springs, and any fasteners separate and recorded. At this point of the disassembly, remove the detent under the top cover in the pattern of the cover-bolt holes if those are used on the model on which you're working.

Some detents have two springs, and they can be held down with screws. If the detent does not have a set screw, the lid will apply pressure, so it will be sticking up above the gasket surface. Remove the screw, spring, and detent. A small, pencil-type magnet can help get the detent out of a deep hole. Removing this one now will help prevent it from falling out and possibly getting lost when you reposition the transmission for further parts removal.

Some Toploaders have two external detent springs that relate to the year they were built. Ford used one spring on 1964–early 1971 models and two springs on late 1971–1973 models. There is one external detent hole on the side of the case near the shift cam lever ports that is for the third/fourth-gear shift rail. This one has a set screw on 1964 to late-1971 cases. On late-1971 to 1973 cases, there will also be a set screw for the first/second-gear shift rail.

All of the external detents use 9/16-inch hex-head bolts. There is one more detent for the reverser, and it needs to be removed inside the case later during disassembly.

Tailhousing and Snap Ring

It is often easier to remove the old tailhousing seal when the tailhousing is still attached to the case so that you can get additional leverage. Inspect this area before disassembly. A special tool can be used to expand and remove the seal easily. Prying out the old seal will destroy it. If you pry out the old seal, take care not to damage any nearby parts, including the output shaft, tailhousing, etc.

Five 5/8-inch hex-head bolts with lock washers hold the tailhousing to the rear of the main case. Remove them and use care when sliding the tailhousing off the output shaft to prevent damage to the plastic speedometer gear and the output shaft.

Some Toploaders have a snap ring securing the speedometer drive gear to the output shaft. It needs to be removed. Later units use a steel clip that holds the speedometer gear in place. Remove the speedometer snap ring or clip from the output shaft.

Speedometer Gear and Ball

With the output shaft still in the case, the builder can use leverage from the output shaft to remove the speedometer gear. With the ring or clip gone, remove the speedometer gear from the shaft. It is plastic, so heat may have seated it on the output shaft. Use a tool to carefully drive it off its location without damaging the output shaft. Take the speedometer-gear drive ball out of its hole in the output shaft. Use a magnet if needed.

Front Bearing Retainer

On the front of the case, remove the four, 1/2-inch hex-head bolts that hold on the input-shaft bearing retainer.

Remove the retainer and its gasket from the input shaft. As this is an external part, it can have corrosion on and inside of it. If this is the case, you

Input-Shaft Removal

The cluster gear must be disengaged from the input shaft before the input shaft can be fully removed. The problem is that there is no way to remove the cluster gear at this point of the disassembly.

The solution is to remove the shaft of the cluster gear. Doing so lowers the cluster gear down and away from the input shaft. With the cluster-gear shaft removed, the cluster gear can then be disengaged from the input shaft. This provides enough clearance movement for the input shaft's engagement teeth to clear the hole in the front of the case and allow removal. ■

may be required to break/destroy the seal of the gasket.

Cluster-Gear Shaft and Input Shaft

Gently drive the cluster-gear shaft rearward and out of the case. Let the cluster gear safely settle to the bottom of the case for now, as it cannot be removed at this time. The cluster gear's needle bearings will likely fall into the case at this point.

Pull the input shaft and its bearings out of the case. Raising the rear of the main case can help keep the 15 needle bearings from falling out of the input shaft. If they do fall out, they should stay inside of the case and fall to the bottom.

Remove the input-shaft snap ring that is in front of the main bearing on the input shaft.

Remove the input-shaft bearing that is one of two main bearings. It needs to be pressed off the input shaft using care to not damage the shaft.

Inside the Case

Remove the set screw from the first/second-gear shift fork (the one toward the rear of the case). Magnets can be used to keep the set screws from falling into the case. All shift-fork set screws have the same 5/32-inch Allen-head bolt. When these are installed, they use a matching angle to seat to the shift rail, which can sometimes make it difficult to remove.

Shift Rails

Remove the first/second-gear shift rail via the hole in the rear of the case. Then, remove the detent that is below it. Use a pencil magnet to get the interlock pin out of the third/fourth shift rail. If you were not able to remove the interlock pin, be careful to not lose it from this point forward. Shift the transmission into third gear for the next step.

Begin this step by removing the third/fourth-gear shift-fork set screw. Lightly tap the inner end of the third/fourth shift rail to force the expansion plug out of its seat on the front of the case. Remove the third/fourth shift rail from the same opening. Be careful not to lose the interlock pin for the shift rail. Interlock pins are similar to detents, as they are location specific and need to be labeled for reuse.

The snap ring is located behind the rear main bearing.

Rear Main Bearing

At this point of disassembly, the builder meets the rear main bearing for the first time. Pressing the rear main bearing on and off the output shaft is the most difficult part of rebuilding a Toploader. Note that using a block of wood and a hammer to remove the rear or front bearing is the absolute worst way to perform this task. Any hammering of the rear main bearing will damage the main shaft, the snap-ring groove for the third/fourth-gear synchronizer, and possibly that synchronizer as well. These are all expensive components to replace.

Alternative methods to using a press or other specialized tools for the rear main and front bearings can be used after the bearings are initially pressed out of their positions. The idea is to polish and hone the contact areas of the bearings (the inside and outside diameters where they apply) so that they become a good hand fit onto the output shaft.

The rear main bearing journal can be polished on the output shaft until the bearing will hand fit. Otherwise,

Allen-Head Bolt Removal

The 5/32-inch Allen-head bolt goes through heat/cool cycles and can be difficult to remove from the shifter fork. If the Allen-head broach opening begins to round out, use a dead-blow hammer to bottom a Torx 27 socket into the hole to achieve maximum contact to turn the screw. Doing this will likely require a new set screw, but it allows the old one to be removed with minimal effort. Avoiding nearby damage saves the shift fork and shift rail. ■

the inside diameter of the bearing can be honed to achieve the same result. When doing this, hone only the inside diameter of the bearing. This can make assembly much easier and faster. In addition, as the builder is now dealing with the rear main bearing for the first time, consider this operation to make the final assembly easier.

This method is not needed for the input shaft's front bearing. The input shaft comes out of the case with the bearing in place, whereas the output shaft will not come out of the case until the bearing is removed. Keep in mind that the input shaft (because of its overall length compared to the output shaft) is much easier to position into a press for pressing bearings.

One way not to deal with pressing off the rear bearing while it is in the case during disassembly is to remove each snap ring from its groove on the output shaft and slide it forward. Then, move the component that is behind it forward to allow access to the next snap ring. Repeat this while the output shaft is still in the case. The output shaft is stepped larger toward the rear of the transmission, and at each position there is a snap ring. Removing a snap ring from its groove and moving it forward allows it to float on the surface in front of it.

The rear main bearing needs to be removed from the output shaft before any of the shift forks can be removed. This bearing is pressed onto the output shaft. Do not try to drive the shaft out of the bearing. It must be pressed off to avoid damaging the output shaft.

Shift Forks and Reverse Shift Rail

Rotate and lift the third/fourth-gear shift fork out of the case. Label the third/fourth-gear shift fork because it is location specific.

Similar to removing the third/fourth-gear shift fork, rotate the first/second-gear shift fork until it can be removed from the case. All three shift forks are dedicated and are not interchangeable. Use a method to identify all three.

With the input gear removed, keep the thrust washer and first gear on the back end of the shaft in place. Then, move the output-shaft assembly up and out of the case by lifting the front of the shaft first. When removed, it should be put aside so that disassembly can continue inside the case. Take care not to damage the output shaft and its components on the edges of the case during removal.

Untighten and remove the reverse shift-fork set screw. Keep the shift fork labeled.

Rotate the reverse shift rail 90 degrees and slide it out through the rear of the case. Note where the detent and spring are located and make contact with the shift rail. They need to go back the same way during assembly.

Reverse Detent Spring and Plug

Use a small magnet to help remove the reverse detent spring and plug. Keep the detent and its spring labeled for reuse. This is the last of the detents to be removed.

Cluster Gear

There is now sufficient clearance for easier removal of the cluster gear. The cluster-gear shaft has four gears on it that do not separate from the assembly. Also remove the cluster gear's roller bearings, which are loose inside of the cluster gear's ends. There are 21 roller bearings on each end of the cluster gear.

As the cluster gear is lifted, the roller bearings could fall out of position and settle to the bottom of the case. Keep these 42 roller bearings separate from any others. There will also be a bearing retainer and thrust washer on each end—note their positioning.

Reverse Countershaft

Gently drive the reverse countershaft rearward out the rear of the case. It can be pushed out with a long screwdriver or a similar tool.

Reverse Idler Gear

The reverse-idler-gear shaft has one straight-cut gear and one helical-cut gear on it, and it should be floating after its shaft has been removed. Also remove the two thrust washers on both ends. Note their location upon removal. Then, remove the 44 needle bearings and their 2 retainers. Check for any needle bearings that may have fallen to the bottom of the case.

Fill Plug

The fill plug is located about halfway up the passenger's side of the case. Removing this will help you drain and clean the inside of the case as thoroughly as possible. This plug is different than the drain plug.

Cam Levers

Pushing the stud from the outside of the case, remove the first/second, third/fourth, and reverse cam levers, making sure that the O-rings are still on the shafts. Keep the forward-gear pieces separate from the reverse piece and label them because they are location and direction specific. These should be the last parts taken out of or off the case.

Output-Shaft Gear Disassembly

With all of the parts out of the case, disassemble the output-shaft gear assembly. Watch for these potential troubled areas while doing so because they are essential for the assembly procedure.

When removing first gear and the first-gear thrust washer from the main shaft, note the direction of the first/second-gear synchronizer and how it needs to mate up. Note the way that it comes off so that it can be reinstalled in the same direction during assembly. The inner hub needs to have the thick side facing the back of the case. The thinner side faces the front.

When removing the first/second-gear synchronizer assembly and snap ring, note the orientation of the first/second gear synchronizer hub. The thinner edge faces second gear, toward the front. When removing second gear, note the orientation of the snap ring and snap-ring spacer.

To disassemble the output-shaft assembly, place it in a position that is comfortable for you to remove its components. If any of the parts are stubborn to remove, never hammer or pry on them. They are not pressed onto the output shaft and should be able to be removed with minimal force. Use the same front-to-back direction and sequence:

Snap Ring

Begin the output-shaft disassembly by removing the snap ring on the front of the output shaft. From the front of the output shaft or by the third/fourth-gear synchronizer, disassemble all of the components by removing the snap ring from the input shaft. Be sure to have a good working position on a flat surface.

Remove the third/fourth-gear synchronizer, blocker ring, and third gear. These easily slide off the output shaft.

Another snap ring needs to be removed to remove the second-gear thrust washer from the shaft. This is the second-gear, tanged thrust washer. This allows second gear to come off the shaft in a forward direction.

First/Second Gear Synchronizer and Blocker Rings

Slide second gear and the blocker ring off the output shaft and note the facing direction of the blocker ring. This allows the first/second-gear synchronizer to come off the shaft in a forward direction. Remove the snap ring on the first/second-gear synchronizer. Then, remove the first/second-gear synchronizer the same way that the gears were removed.

Slide the thrust washer, first gear, and the blocker ring off the output shaft and note the direction of the blocker ring. First gear can come off the shaft from either direction, but the thrust washer only comes off from the rear. These are the last pieces to come off the output shaft for disassembly.

Synchronizer Disassembly

The synchronizer disassembly sequence includes multiple counts of C-springs (four) and two different sets of three keys (or "dogs") that are parts of the synchronizer.

Most of the original factory synchronizers were marked with an etch mark on their back side. Thoroughly inspect yours. If no marks are found, make some on the parts if you are planning to reuse them. Wear patterns are created with use, and parts work better when they are rematched. You may already know this from reinstalling an engine's cam and lifters.

As with synchronizers themselves, the components of a synchronizer are particular to that synchronizer and its location. Most of the parts from the first/second-gear synchronizer will not work in the third/fourth-gear synchronizer. Specifically, the inner and outer hubs and dogs are dedicated to each synchronizer. The only items that can interchange are the C-springs.

This completes the disassembly of a Toploader. Remember to keep all of the parts organized after cleaning and inspection—even those that you plan to replace. Until the complete unit has been assembled and road tested, it is best to keep all of the parts labeled and organized. Many parts of a Toploader look the same or very similar when, in fact, they are not.

The pointer shows where most of the visible wear will appear on a first/second-gear synchronizer inner hub gear. Many of the parts of the two synchronizers are not interchangeable. The straight-cut gear on the outside of a first/second-gear synchronizer is used for reverse gearing. (Photo Courtesy David Randal)

Remember that most of the synchronizer's parts are dedicated and will not fit the other synchronizer. Note how this dog fits into the gear. (Photo Courtesy David Randal)

INSPECTION

David Kee has a solid reputation for building and rebuilding Toploaders. With thousands of them being built and rebuilt in his shop, he's seen patterns in which parts and assemblies typically need to be replaced. He provided a list of the top troubled spots to check for when inspecting a Toploader so that builders can avoid the common pitfalls. From each item on his list, I provided the problem, how to accurately inspect for it, and the solution.

Bearing Retainer Diameter in the Bellhousing

Good fitment between the bellhousing and the bearing retainer on the front of the case is essential to the alignment of the two parts. Any misalignment can cause balance and additional wear problems to several components. Jumping out of gear, clutch chatter, and difficult shifting can occur. In 1964, Ford used $4^{11}/_{16}$-inch-diameter bearing retainers. In 1965-and-newer models, Ford used $4^{7}/_{8}$-inch-diameter bearing retainers.

One of the best ways to check parts is to compare the part that is potentially damaged with an undamaged part. The damaged input gear (right) has numerous issues. Note the scoring and glazing on the cone area. In addition, note the worn engagement teeth and how they are reduced in size. Finally, the large gear teeth show chipping on the leading edge and are generally worn down in areas where they are normally sharp. (Photo Courtesy David Kee)

Inspection

Accurately measure the inside diameter (ID) of the bellhousing and the outside diameter (OD) of the bearing retainer. The two pieces should fit hand tight, as they are almost the same measurement. Try fitting the bearing retainer to the bellhousing before it has been installed on the transmission.

Solution

If the bellhousing's opening is too large, that proper fit is impossible to obtain. It may signify that the bellhousing is beyond tolerance and may need to be replaced. The cost of repairing the bore and keeping it centered would be more difficult and/or costly than finding another bellhousing.

Cracks Around the Bearing-Retainer Bolt Holes

The four holes holding the bearing retainer onto the case are subjected to a tremendous amount of torque from the bellhousing bolting up to the engine and transmission. With two engine mounts and one

A typical bearing retainer is a cast-iron piece with a critical outside diameter that fits tightly into the hole in the bellhousing. This prevents vibration from the transmission not being centered behind the crankshaft.

transmission mount, engine torque twists the bellhousing, and that transfers to the bearing retainer. The four holes are at the end of that torque, and cracks may form at the holes. Kee believes that these cracks are caused by the continuous forward and backward thrust of the helical gears. Over time, all of that pressure on such a small area can cause cracks.

Inspection

Clean the bearing retainer vigorously and inspect around each hole. Use magnification and plenty of light to look for small cracks that are starting.

Solution

If cracks are present, the bearing retainer must be replaced. Otherwise, it will leak gear lube into the clutch compartment.

Bearing Retainer Length on $1^{3}/_{8}$-Inch Input Shaft

The length of the bearing retainer is important to allow clearance for aftermarket clutch discs to match properly to the bellhousing. Ford used a thin clutch-disc hub and made the $1^{3}/_{8}$-inch bearing retainers a little longer than the smaller-spline units.

Inspection

Measure the overall length of the bearing retainer. Do not use it if this measurement is more than 3½ inches.

Solution

Most aftermarket clutch hubs are thicker than stock clutch hubs, so be sure that the bearing retainer isn't taller than 3½ inches. This way, if the clutch is changed in the future, there will be no interference problems. If the retainer is left longer, it will apply pressure on the inner hub and force the clutch disc against the flywheel when the transmission is bolted to the bellhousing, causing numerous problems. In the worst-case scenario, the mounting ears of the case can break. If the bearing retainer is more than 3½ inches long, it needs to be exchanged or machined down to 3½ inches.

Input Pilot Bushing Surface Length

The input shaft needs to be the proper length to support the pilot bushing. If the length of its surface

A typical bearing retainer is shown before a rebuild. Just because the bearing retainer is located inside the bellhousing with the clutch does not mean that it is safe from road debris. In fact, there will likely be debris, as clutch material is ground during normal use. Debris can make it difficult to find cracks around the bolt holes.

is not adequate, the shaft will not be supported properly and will be allowed to move, likely causing imbalance and wear. Jumping out of gear, clutch chatter, and difficult shifting can occur. In the worst-case scenario if the input shaft is not supported by the pilot bushing, the front bearing in the transmission will fail. This causes damage to the input-shaft gear, cluster gear, case, and output shaft.

Never use an extended pilot bushing in a small-block application and run a big-block input shaft. If this is done, the part of the pilot bushing that is contacting the input shaft hangs outside the crank pocket and the pilot bushing becomes loose.

Kee said, "I have seen grown men almost in tears when they see the damage that this causes and how costly it will be to repair all the damaged parts."

Inspection

Install the pilot bushing/bearing and measure the length.

Solution

Use the correct-length input shaft behind a small-block and double-check the length prior to assembly. Make sure that the input shaft will reach all the way into the pilot bushing. On big-blocks, make sure that the pilot bushing area is not too long, bottoming out in the crankshaft's pocket. This is normally not a problem unless a small-block transmission is installed on a big-block.

Twist in the Input-Shaft Splines

The input shaft receives a tremendous amount of torque. As the input shaft wears, the splines are the first to show the wear with a noticeable twist in the splines. This applies to both sizes of input shafts ($1^1/_{16}$- and $1^3/_8$-inch models) and is more rare in the $1^3/_8$-inch input shafts.

Inspection

Even if it does not look like the spline teeth are twisted to the naked eye, those conditions may be just beginning to occur. This can be best tested by inserting the shaft into a clutch disc. If the disc cannot move easily up and down the entire input-shaft spline, twisting may be present.

Solution

A new input shaft may be needed.

Twist in the Output-Shaft Splines

Similar to the input shaft, wear and torque can cause the spline teeth on an output shaft to begin to twist. The next step would be the output shaft twisting in half.

The spline on an input shaft must be straight and undamaged. Checking for twisted splines is as easy as putting the shaft into a clutch disc to check for smoothness, drag, and any resistance. If the fitment between the two pieces is not smooth, the input shaft may need to be replaced.

This input shaft shows typical wear that is usually harmless—as long as the spline is still true. Sometimes, that wear can hide a twisted spline, so check it with a clutch disc.

Inspection

Test with a yoke to ensure that the splined part of the yoke passes all the way over the splines on the shaft until it bottoms out. As with the input shaft, even if it does not look like the spline teeth are twisted to the naked eye, those conditions may just be starting to occur.

With a visual inspection, the driveshaft spline on a Toploader's output shaft doesn't always indicate twisting. The best way to test for this is to couple the spline with a matching driveshaft yoke to make sure that the two splines work together all the way up each spline.

Solution

If the yoke does not want to fully engage and bottom out, replacement of the output shaft is suggested.

Tailhousing Shifter Location

Ford used six different shifter locations on its 11 different tailhousing designs. Some used various casting bosses with bolt holes drilled, tapped, or left blank. Others moved the shifter several inches from front to back.

Inspection

Verify the tailhousing casting numbers for the application that is being built. If the tailhousing was removed from the same car that it

Run the output shaft all the way into the driveshaft yoke and watch (and feel) for drag and rough spots as well as if the yoke will fully accept the input-shaft splines. If the yoke does not allow full fitment along the output shaft, the problem may be a twisted spline. The solution is to use a new output shaft to keep the union from flexing and prevent damage to other key internal parts. (Photo Courtesy David Randal)

A: *13 5/8 inches to handle at floor; 19 5/8 inches at knob. Vehicles: 1964–1965 Comet, Falcon, and Ranchero.*
B: *16¼ inches to handle at floor; 20¼ inches at knob. Vehicles: 1964–1967 Galaxie.*
C: *18 inches to handle at floor; 20 inches at knob. Vehicles: 1966–1970 Fairlane and Torino.*
D: *20¾ inches to handle at floor; 22¾ inches at knob. Vehicles: 1964–1973 Mustang; 18 3/8 inches to knob for the 427 Cobra.*

When locating the shifter mounting points, David Kee's chart for the front face of the Toploader's case yields these measurements. If the shifter plate being used does not match the specifications, it may not be the correct one. (Photo Courtesy David Kee)

is going back into, it should match up. If the Toploader has come from another source, reference the "Tailhousing Codes" table in chapter 2 for the correct specifications.

Solution

Be sure that the tailhousing has the correct shifter location for the application. Note that the correct shifter mounting plate can be used to move the shifter to the correct location. In other situations, a new tailhousing that generates the correct measurements may be needed.

Wear in the Key Slots on the Inner Hubs of Synchronizer Assemblies

The key slots provide a good fit for the keys to position themselves to join the two gears and hold the C-springs. The keys also interface with the outer hubs, helping them to correctly distribute energy throughout the synchronizer assembly.

If the key slots have excessive wear, the blocker-ring engagement teeth can rotate enough to block the outer synchronizer hub from sliding over to the gear. This will keep the transmission from shifting into that gear easily. Lowering the RPM and double or triple clutching while trying to select that gear will be the only way to get the hub to slide past the blocker ring.

Inspection

Inspect wear in the key locations in the inner hubs. Inspect the keys. Replace the keys if they show any deformation of their shape.

Solution

If wear is found in the inner hubs, replacement is suggested. The inner and outer hubs should be replaced in pairs to ensure proper fitment and functionality.

The inner-hub wear is clear on both sides of the long teeth of this inner synchronizer for third/fourth gear. Note how the wear is one direction on one side of the teeth and the other direction on the other side of the teeth. This happens because the slider is driving each gear halfway onto the hub. When hubs are worn this much, they are notchy when sliding the outer hub back and forth. This photo shows how the slot for the dog is also worn. (Photo Courtesy David Kee)

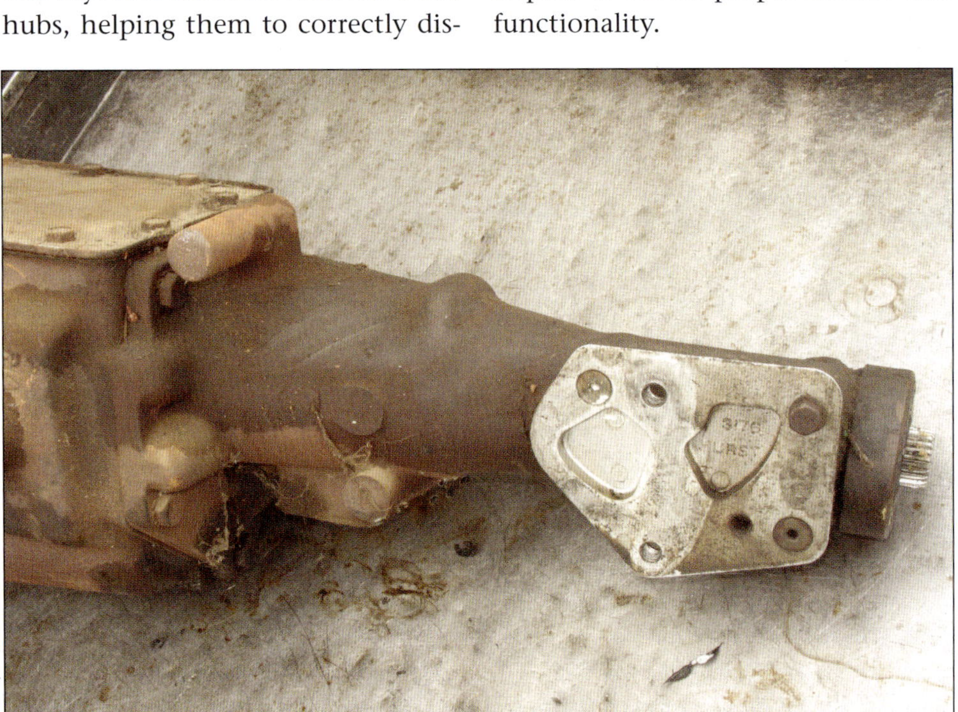

When checking the shifter mounting points for fitment to the application, keep in mind that alignment problems can also be caused by having the wrong shifter plate bolted onto the tailhousing. This photo shows a Hurst shifter plate in place on a Toploader.

Loose Pins in the Cam and the Shafts

The pins that contact the shift fork are pressed into the cam flats and can sometimes begin to work themselves loose. This movement affects how they interact with the shift forks.

Inspection

Inspect for partial and full cracks that allow movement of the pin within the flats. Also assess the alignment of the pin within the hole.

Solution

Replacement is one option. On the back side of the pin are four tabs that wedge the pin in place. Firmly tapping on them with a hammer while the pin is on a firm surface tightens the pins in place. A more permanent solution is to tungsten inert gas (TIG) weld the pin to the flat with a few well-spaced tack welds or even weld all the way around the junction. Take care to not heat-warp the piece because alignment can be affected. All of the new cams and shafts coming from David Kee are TIG welded before being heat treated, which eliminates any chance of the pin coming loose.

Excessive Wear on the Coast Side of the Engagement Teeth

On the coast side of the engagement teeth of every forward-speed gear are six teeth that are wider than the others. Three of them should be shiny from wear, and straight across from them are three more. These are important because they keep the transmission from slipping out of gear on light deceleration. If all of the teeth are shiny on the coast side of the engagement teeth, replace the gear.

These are examples of OEM (bottom) and modified cam and shaft pieces. The OEM part shows the pin pressed and peened over to secure it in the lever. The top one has been welded to ensure no movement of the pin. (Photo Courtesy David Randal)

Bellhousing Alignment

The bellhousing alignment for all manual transmissions is important. Anything that can disrupt the flow of engine energy to the flywheel, clutch, and transmission has an increasing effect on the balance of those components and how effectively they operate. In addition to balance, fitment also comes into play. A misaligned bellhousing can be misfit to the engine, and that can also contribute to breaking case ears during installation.

Inspection

Inspect all of the mounting holes for elongation of the hole that the bolts pass through as well as the threaded holes in the block. In addition, check for any burrs or high spots on the bellhousing flange on the engine block. Check the spacer plate on both sides for defects in the areas that contact the engine block and bellhousing. Check the flange on the bellhousing that meets the space plate as well as the face of the bellhousing that contacts the transmission. Finally, check the face of the transmission that meets the bellhousing.

It doesn't take much to damage these components. Bumping the edge of any of the surfaces against a hard surface or even the edge of a bench can put a nick in the edge. That nick may cause a high spot on the edge of the face. This type of flaw can normally be seen or felt. Using a fine file over all of the surfaces will reveal damage. Another factor could be an uneven buildup of paint on mating surfaces.

When painting a Toploader, know which mating surfaces will and won't be affected by coats of primer and paint. This builder opted for a gloss-black finish on this Toploader but masked off the flange on the front of the case. The gasket surface for the top cover is also free of paint and will provide a great seal for the cover's gasket.

Bellhousing alignment issues can be caused by many factors. Nicks and contact marks on the face of the front flange of the case (seen here) are some of those factors. These nicks and marks can cause high spots in the face of the case, throwing off the alignment enough to cause balancing problems.

Shift forks wear on the inside of the curve where they contact the synchronizers. It is usually not possible to determine whether the fork has excessive wear with the naked eye. Measure the forks to determine the wear level and if replacement is required. (Photo Courtesy David Randal)

Measuring the pads on the shift forks is an effective way to determine how much life is left in those parts. Applying to both sets of forward-gear shift forks, this photo shows a pad to be about 0.301 inch and undersized. (Photo Courtesy David Randal)

Solution

Most aftermarket bellhousing manufacturers have a procedure for alignment that is readily available and usually easily adaptable to other bellhousings. Many repair manuals also have instructions for checking bellhousing alignment.

Shift Fork Wear in the Cam Slots

Contact between the cam lever and the shift fork occurs during every shift. Misalignment (even a small amount) can start excessive wear. Normal use can also create wear.

Inspection

Perform a thorough visual inspection on the cam slots of the shift fork for obvious heavy indentations.

Solution

Replacement of the shift fork is suggested if it is heavily damaged.

Shift Fork Thickness

Expect to see shift fork wear where it engages the synchronizer. Much like brake drums and rotors, there are minimum thicknesses for the engagement portion of the shift fork.

Check the pads on the first/second- and third/fourth-gear shift forks. New shift forks measure 0.345 inch. When they are worn down to 0.310 inch or less, replacement is suggested.

Front Bearing Bore Alignment

If the front main bearing is not holding its position, the entire driveline of input and output shafts will move out of alignment. This can throw off tolerances for every part that works with those two shafts, which includes

This photo shows the measurement of a new shift fork's pad with a 0.345-inch measurement. That size is within the working tolerances for a Toploader shift fork's pad and can be safely used in a build. (Photo Courtesy David Randal)

almost every part of a Toploader. Any parts that are then misaligned can wear or break prematurely.

Inspection

Measure the inside diameter of the front bearing hole in the case and the outside diameter of the front bearing. The front bearing should be a hand fit in the case with minimal to no rocking. If the bearing rocks in the bore, examine the bore for marks from the outer race spinning.

Solution

Replace the case or have the bore sleeved back to the original dimension.

Parts Inspection

The tips above were intentionally placed at the beginning of this chapter so that a builder can easily reference them during the inspection process. Now that a builder knows where to expect trouble, it's time for a thorough parts inspection.

Clean and inspect every part of the transmission. Within the 244 parts that comprise a Toploader, none are unimportant and all warrant an inspection.

Much like the old saying, "garbage in, garbage out," what goes into building a Toploader will affect how well or how poorly it operates. The most important thing is to be consistent in the inspection stage. Be thorough and don't approve a piece unless you are 100-percent sure and comfortable with that decision. This includes all new pieces going into the build as well. Just because a part is new doesn't mean that it will fit and work correctly. New parts warrant inspection not only in condition but also in size, fit, and function.

I'm going to follow the disassembly sequence for this inspection chapter. As always, learning disassembly in sequence can help in the assembly procedure because they are similar. I suggest checking all of the parts, including those that you plan to replace, because knowing where any related damage is found can lead to the cause of that damage. This can reduce or eliminate trouble down the line.

After cleaning and removing all old gasket material and seals, inspect the following parts.

Top Cover and Bolts

Check the top cover for corrosion, warpage, and/or elongation of the 10 holes. In addition, look for rust-through and thin spots. Unlike most of the other parts of a Toploader, the cover is a simple steel stamping, and since it is exposed to under-car conditions, it can easily rust. The cover's normal resting position is horizontal, and it contains edges and surfaces that can retain water and other corrosion-inducing materials from the road. The probability is good that the top cover will need to be replaced.

If you are using the OEM vent, make sure that the hole in the cover

Test Fitting Is Beneficial

Test fit all of the parts and assemblies before installing them into an assembly for the final build. This can be done when all parts have been inspected and are being laid out for assembly. Test fitting is especially beneficial when lining up the detent pins that are used on shift rails. Many of those parts are designed for only one location and do not work in other locations.

Another perk for the builder during inspection is having more time to learn where and how all of the Toploader's pieces work together. Performing a "dry fit" to see how certain pieces work together ensures that they will work when assembly is complete and those 10 bolts are finally holding down the cover. ■

Part of a good inspection is knowing that everything is ready to work correctly for assembly. Using a tap to ensure the threads for the cover bolts and for a detent retainer is thorough preparation. Take care to make sure that if any additional threading is needed, all chips and related waste is properly removed before final assembly. (Photo Courtesy David Randal)

is not clogged and remains open. Inspect the bolts for damage on both the threads and hex heads. The bolts are 1/2-inch, serrated-flange, hex-head bolts. Inspect their threads and the hex heads for damage.

There are 10 bolts that hold down the cover. There is also one hole that is used for the first/second-gear detent (and/or spring if used on that model). Make sure to keep all detents, springs, and fasteners marked regarding where they go because they are not interchangeable.

Detents and Springs

Look for burrs, worn spots, and wear on the detents. Then, check the springs for any collapsing, bends, or breaks in the wires. Keep all detents labeled so that they go back to their correct locations in the proper way. Detents are similar in appearance but are not interchangeable. The fasteners that hold the detents in place should be checked for thread and head damage. Holes in the case can be checked later when that component is checked.

Third/Fourth-Gear Detent Bolt

Check the threads and contact points for wear and damage. This bolt is located outside the main case on the driver's side by the cams and the shafts. Check the hex head for wear. Since the bolt is on the outside of the case, it is subject to under-car weathering and corrosion.

Shift-Fork Set Screws

The shift-fork set screws hold the shift forks to the shift rails, so make sure that the set screws are in working condition and their threads and contact points are not damaged. The set screws are angled on the end and match up with a similar angle on the shift rail for the strongest connection possible. As they are sometimes hard

The set screws in the shift forks have an Allen head, and sometimes that head gets chewed up during removal. Make sure to inspect the set screw for a properly shaped hole. All three set screws are the same size, so keeping them separate is not required.

The tailhousing is held in place with five standard bolts that are interchangeable, so keeping them separate is not required. Inspect the two cast-iron pieces of the case and tailhousing for damage, including the threads and holes themselves.

The speedometer parts include the gear, snap ring or clip, and check ball. If you are using a speedometer, the build requires these parts. Shown here are the gear and snap ring during the removal of the ring. The ball is located under the gear.

to separate, make sure that the contacting points are in good shape.

Check the Allen-head openings of the screws to make sure that they still function properly. If any of the screws received damage during disassembly, ascertain whether they can be used again or if they need to be replaced. These three set screws are all the same size.

On the front of the case, check the bearing retainer, the bearing, its opening, and the groove for the snap ring. All must be free of any damage. The snap ring should be flat and not racked in any way.

Tailhousing and Bolts

These five bolts can make wear patterns in the holes, depending on how many times the housing has been removed and installed. Check the holes in the tailhousing casting for elongation and damage from the bolts and washers. Check the bolts for damage on the threads and hex heads.

Speedometer Gear, Snap Ring/Clip, and Check Ball

Check the plastic speedometer gear for cracks, chips, and excessive wear on all internal and external surfaces. Check the rest of the pieces for wear and functionality. Make sure that whatever type of gear retainer (snap ring or clip) is used, it is still operable for the rebuild. David Kee recommends switching to a snap ring and ball because the clips can come loose and allow the speedometer gear to move down the shaft and cause the speedometer gear to stop working.

Front Bearing Retainer and Snap Ring on Input Shaft

Check all holes for elongation and that the snap ring itself is not

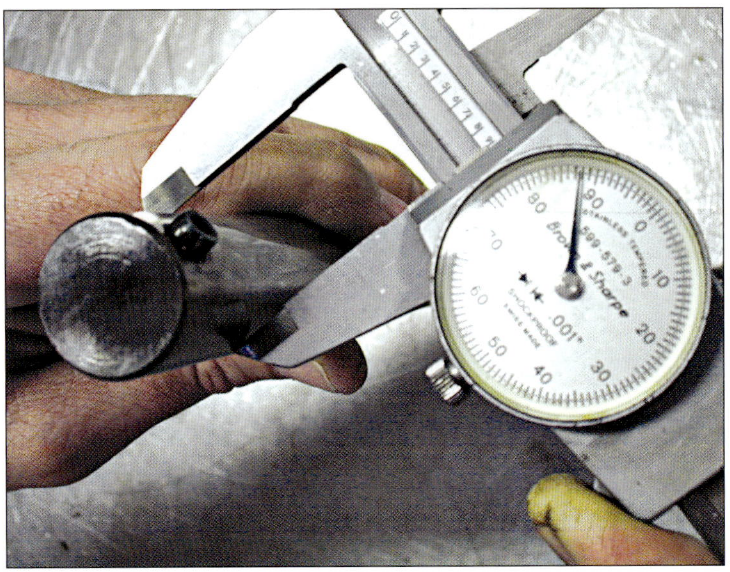

Check the outside diameter of the countershafts. Measure them in numerous places along their length for consistency and possible bends. The best way to check for tolerance is to install them into the case they will end up in. If they fit where they contact the cast-iron bores of the case with no slop or bind, they are okay to use. (Photo Courtesy David Randal)

racked and is still good. Input-shaft bearings are another common area for trouble. As they are located under the retainer, corrosion can get inside and corrode the bearings before the internal pieces. Bearing retainer length on 1^3/$_8$-inch input shafts needs to be 3½ inches overall. The stock ones are longer and often bottom out on aftermarket clutch-disc hubs.

If you are working on a transmission with a 1^3/$_8$-inch input shaft, look at the leading edge of the sleeve on which the throwout bearing slides. If there is scoring, the disc has been contacting that point. In addition, inspect the bearing retainer for cracks at the bolt holes from the hole inward to the bearing snap-ring groove. Make sure that the snap-ring groove ring is clean and not deformed.

First/Second-Gear Shift Rail

The first/second-gear shift rail is one of three shift rails, so check all of them for wear, abrasions, and any bending. The best way to check for trueness is to put each rail in a lathe to check runout with a dial indicator. Label each shift rail and its placement. Also note the direction needed for reassembly.

Another aspect is the diameter of the rails, especially where they are riding in the bores of the case. The best way to check the fitment of a shift rail is to install it into the boss of the same case that it will end up in during assembly. If a shift rail fits into its boss with no sloppiness or binding, it is the correct size.

Cluster Gear

The cluster gear is one of the most complex pieces in a Toploader. Check the cluster gear for runout at various locations along its shaft. Inspect all gears for wear, chips, and the condition of the teeth. In addition, look for signs of any heat damage or discoloration. The inside diameter of the cluster gear should also be checked for damage. Look where the roller bearings will seat. It should be a smooth surface with no abrasions or galling. In addition, check the shaft on which the cluster gear rides for wear and runout.

Inspect the thrust washers at each end of the cluster-gear shaft for wear, even if they will be replaced. The roll pin and its hole used on the cluster gear should also be checked for wear and damage and to ensure that they will work together properly.

Check the oil holes for any blockages, as the simple lubrication system of a Toploader is critical. Double-check that the cluster gear going into the build is compatible with the gears that will be used. This is especially true when changing from wide to close gears or vice versa.

Inspecting the cluster gear includes the gear, its 42 needle bearings, 2 needle-bearing retainers, and 2 metallic thrust washers. Check the condition of each part as well as the fitment of all parts when assembled. (Photo Courtesy David Randal)

Cluster-Gear Needle Bearings

Count and check the 42 cluster-gear needle bearings for wear, discoloration, straightness, and damage. Again, perform this inspection even if you are replacing the needle bearings. Finding wear in a replaced part can indicate other problems in related components that need to be discovered and corrected. If new roller bearings are to be used, a test fit into position will confirm readiness.

Input Shaft

Check for damage and wear on the gear and engagement teeth. Inspect the wear patterns for unusual markings. Inspect the 15 needle bearings that are located inside the input shaft for wear, straightness, and damage. If new needle bearings are to be used, a test fit into position will confirm readiness.

Verify that the input shaft is correct for the engine if the transmission did not come out of that car. There are two sizes, and they were used the same for wide- and close-ratio models. The smaller one is $1^{1}/_{16}$ inches in diameter and the larger one is $1^{3}/_{8}$ inches in diameter. The length is critical too. Big-block engines require a 3/4-inch-length pilot-bushing surface. Small-block engines require a 1¼-inch-length pilot-bushing surface. Originally, the larger spline was only available for big-blocks.

Check the input-shaft splines for wear and twisting. Test fit the clutch disc to be sure that the disc splines can freely travel the entire distance of the splines. If the disc only travels so far and stops, you may have a twisted input shaft.

An input shaft has many items to check to ensure readiness for assembly, including the splines, a gear, engagement teeth, a cone, numerous bearing surfaces, and straightness. Begin by making sure that it is the correct input shaft to be used with the engine.

To properly install the main bearing, which is one of two that are used, begin with inspecting the bore in the case for measurement/tolerance of the pressed-in bearing. Then, the bearing and its snap ring hold everything in position. Inspect each bearing for moving bearing races and cage integrity.

Input-Shaft Bearing

Check the input-shaft bearing bore to make sure that there is no evidence of the bearing race spinning in the case. When a front bearing wears excessively, its cage can break open and allow all of the balls to go to one side. The fragments of the cage and the ball bearings can jam and cause the outer race to spin in the case. If the bore is damaged or the bearing rocks in the bore, the case must be repaired or replaced.

Main Bearings

Many builders inspect both bearings at the same time to help with consistency. These bearings are pressed on and off the input and output shafts and should be inspected, even if they are to be replaced. Make sure that all roller bearings are still intact with no loose balls and are in working order. Do the inside and outside races move too much on the ball bearings? Check all friction surfaces on the shafts for wear and abrasions.

Shift Forks

Inspect all shift forks for cracks, heat checking where they engage the slider. Watch for galling and hot spots. The pads that ride in the synchronizers are 0.345 inch thick when they are new. Minor wear is acceptable. Major wear is indicated by a thickness of less than 0.315 inch. Since a shift fork moves for each shift, replacing worn shift forks is highly recommended.

Reverse Idler Shift Rail

Note the condition of the shaft's surface as well as the ends of the shaft for wear and damage.

This shows two of the three shift forks that are used. As they affect the movement in and out of the gears that they change, they are subjected to numerous forces. Check them for cracks and especially for the correct pad sizing. (Photo Courtesy David Randal)

Inspecting the shifter cams and levers includes making sure that the O-ring grooves are intact and free of defects that would damage the rubber O-ring. A faulty O-ring may cause leaking lubricant from the three bores in the side of the case. (Photo Courtesy David Randal)

The reverse idler shift rail is complex. Inspect the gears and splines, the bores for the needle bearings, and how the gears move and slide on the shaft. Look for chafing on the ends if the metallic thrust washers are heavily damaged.

Reverse Gears

There are two gears on the reverse-gear shaft. Look for broken or chipped teeth and inspect the inside diameters for wear patterns and/or damage. Make sure that they can move on the shaft easily. Check the faces too.

Shifter Cams and Levers

The shifter cams and levers are the last pieces to be removed from the case. Inspect the cams and shafts for cracks where the shift levers bottom out on the shaft. Sometimes, the shift-lever nuts are overtightened and the flat areas between the shift lever and the O-ring can crack. The flat part of the cam should be perfectly flat to maintain clearance for the port of the case through which the shaft travels. If the transmission was removed from a running car, the cams and levers should be in place. If the transmission was bought to rebuild and does not have shift levers on it, this needs to be checked.

The easiest way to check for this during teardown is to pull out on each threaded section of the shaft and determine if the flat part of the shift lever bottoms out on and is protruding from the case. If you are not sure, bolt a shift lever onto each one and make sure that it rotates easily. If it does not rotate when you take the cam and shaft out, you will see that the flat part is bent—likely from something hitting the shaft and pushing it in until it bottomed out on the fork inside. This is common on transmissions that have changed hands a few times.

David Kee has seen transmissions that were shipped without this vulnerable area protected, and sometimes all three cams have been bent. The small button that rides in the fork is a wedge fit, and it may come loose. Tapping the back of the pin will often tighten it up. If there is excessive wear on the diameter of the button where it contacts the fork, replace the assembly.

Another area to check with the shift levers and cams is the groove in the shaft for the O-ring. The groove is deep, helping the O-ring to seat deeper and better. The groove needs to be free of any abrasions, cuts, and burrs so that the rubber O-ring is not damaged. The shift levers and cams

Shifter cam levers are simple in appearance but include numerous functions that require thorough checking. Check the shafts, buttons, O-ring grooves, and threads for proper sizing and functionality. Check the tightness of the pins to the flats for fitment. (Photo Courtesy David Randal)

Welding Solution

Builders of high-performance Toploaders often tack weld the button of the cam and lever piece to the flat piece. This ensures that it does not move out of its position. From the factory, that connection was press-fit together, and under heavy-duty conditions, it can become loose. Welding prevents the pieces from coming loose. ■

go through openings in the side of the case, and the O-rings keep the lubricant in the transmission from leaking out those openings.

The Case

The case needs a thorough, inside-and-out inspection. Look for wear, damage, and bolt holes that may need to be cleaned out, chased, or re-tapped. This should be the builder's first contact with any threaded holes and a good habit to begin at this time is to chase the threads of all such holes. Previous builders may have used the wrong chemicals on threaded holes, and they may need cleaning. Check all of the threaded holes to make sure that they are clean and functioning for final assembly.

Look at the gasket and mating areas that have been machined because they may need to be trued or resurfaced. These same areas can be subjected to scratches and gouges when the old gaskets are removed.

This is also the time to look for cracks in locations such as the corners and around all holes. Inside the case, look at the bosses where the shift rails mount. Make sure that they are not chipped, damaged, or excessively worn.

Check the holes for the cluster gear and reverse shafts for size and smoothness. On the outside of the case, clean the cast surface and look for cracks at all junction points and ports because the case has been exposed to various road conditions.

At this point, all parts have been removed from the case, including the output shaft with most of its components (attached or not). Watch for the areas with potential issues.

Output-shaft removal likely includes the rest of the gears and synchronizers that ride on that shaft. There are more parts than meet the

There are many items to check when inspecting the case. All bores, holes, threaded holes, gasket surfaces, and flat mounting surfaces need to be inspected for trueness, and the seating areas inside and out need examination. If a specification or size is unknown, this is the time to make sure that it's correct.

Due to the straight-cut gears on the outside, this assembled synchronizer is easily identified as the one for first and second gear. Another difference between the two synchronizers is the inner hub's diameters. The larger inside diameter belongs to the first- and second-gear synchronizer.

eye on this assembly. In addition, at this point, the orientation of parts is critical, so keep them in order as you take them apart. For inspection of the components on the output shaft, keep the following points in mind.

Synchronizers

Keep the synchronizers separate and disassemble them. To take them apart, compress and remove the C-springs, and the rest of the pieces come apart easily.

Each synchronizer consists of nine parts: one for the inner hub, one for the outer hub, three synchronizer keys (sometimes called dogs), two bronze rings, and two C-springs. Some synchronizer parts are particular to their specific assembly, even though they may look almost identical.

If the synchronizer keys are switched, chaos would ensue. There is a slight difference between the two sets of keys, and the first/second-gear keys are slightly longer. Other parts that are dedicated to a particular synchronizer are the inner and outer hubs. These hubs and keys will not interchange between the two synchronizers and should also be kept separate and labeled.

The C-springs and bronze blocker rings are all the same within the two synchronizers. They can be swapped if needed. Inspect all teeth on the inside and outside of the hubs and blocker rings, the bores of the hubs, the condition of the synchronizer keys, and the working order of the C-springs by checking them for flatness.

- Inspect all synchronizer key slots because they can have wear that is not easily seen. In addition, keys can become dislodged, letting the synchronizer ring rotate too far, causing block-out shifting. When these areas are worn, replacement of the first/second- and third/fourth-gear synchronizers is required.
- As the gears are inspected, remember that if a gear needs to be replaced, the associated synchronizer also must be replaced. Double-check the cluster gear, especially where the faulty gear meshes. If the gear needs to be replaced because of worn engagement teeth, replace the associated synchronizer as well.
- On the subject of gears, worn teeth on the second and third gears is a common problem. The bonus of replacing them is that today's replacement gears often come with longer teeth. This helps engagement. In addition, finding worn synchronizer engagement teeth is common.

The engagement teeth on a slider that slide over the blocker ring and engage second gear are shown. The teeth show wear. They should be sharp and pointed. Inspect both sides of the sliders on all forward gears.

Gears, Rings, Snap Rings, Washers, and the Output Shaft

There are 32 parts on the output shaft, including the shaft itself. I broke them down into two lists: 1) the gears and related parts, rings, snap rings, and washers, and 2) the output shaft itself. Note that the part names will repeat, as some of these parts are the same.

Beginning from the front of the output shaft, inspect the following parts from the first group.

Checklist #1

1. Input-shaft snap ring: Check for flatness, cracks, and chips.
2. Bearing snap ring: Check for flatness.
3. Front bearing: Check ball bearings and the inside and outside of the races and surfaces.
4. Output shaft: The most important component in a Toploader is the output shaft. Because it is the "heart" of a Toploader and almost all of the other parts work off it in one fashion or another, its components and operation are critical.

    Check the output shaft for damage, scoring, heat marks, and any broken edges as the shaft changes diameters. Check oil passages and travel grooves for debris and ensure that they are open and unrestricted. On the wide areas where the synchronizers travel, check for any abrasions as well as all smooth surfaces.

    On the second- and third-gear journals, there is a thrust surface that runs against the gear. Check these surfaces for wear, heat marks, and galling. Check each of the output-shaft splines for wear, damage, twisting, and cracking.

The "heart" of a Toploader, the output shaft, contains almost every gear, and its motion is used to turn the driveshaft. The various dimension steps are for gears, synchronizers, snap rings, and fitting the input shaft. Note the channels for lubrication travel.

This is the location on the output shaft for the first/second-gear synchronizer and where it rides on long teeth. The area that is indicated on the left shows where smaller teeth extensions have been broken off next to the snap-ring groove. Heat discoloration is present. The area that is indicated on the right shows the front edge of the other snap-ring groove, which has broken off. These conditions could cause difficulty for second gear moving on and off the shaft. (Photo Courtesy David Randal)

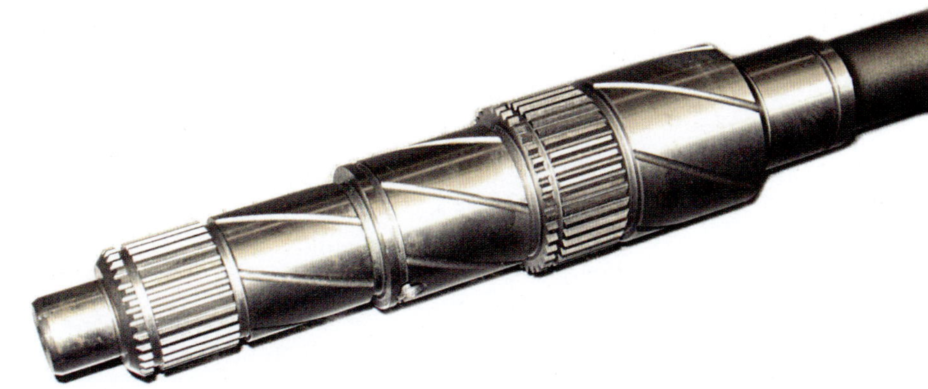

The front of an output shaft shows the longer splines for the first/second-gear and third/fourth-gear synchronizer as well as the smaller splines on the leading edges of those areas. This is another critical area to inspect because previous building/rebuilding may have damaged those smaller spline ends.

Rust pitting damage on the front tip of the output shaft often comes from moisture in a transmission that may have been sitting outside or in an unprotected environment. Although this damage seems light, this output shaft should be replaced.

Placing the output shaft in a lathe to check for true is a great way to determine if it has any runout, which can cause multiple problems for almost any component that attaches to the shaft. Locate the shaft into the jaws of the lathe, taking care to line it up as straight as possible. Once the shaft is straight in the lathe, use a dial indicator to read the front of the shaft for runout. (Photo Courtesy David Randal)

In addition, check the condition of the spline that couples with the driveshaft at the back end. Look for any lateral distortion or twisting of the spline teeth. Test fit the driveshaft yoke to be sure that the yoke can freely travel until it bottoms out on the shaft. If the yoke only travels so far and stops, you may have a twisted output shaft.

The front of the output shaft is where third gear and its synchronizer reside. Make sure that all dimensions are accurate with no broken edges. Check the spline at the very front, as that engages what the third/fourth-gear synchronizer fits onto. The splines past the snap-ring groove for the third/fourth-gear synchronizer may get chipped off and not allow the snap ring to seat properly.

5. Needle bearings: There are 15 needle bearings for the input shaft. Check them for trueness, wear, and any abrasions.
6. Bronze blocker rings: Bronze is often used as a sacrificial material, and these pieces wear faster than others. Thoroughly check all of the teeth, the inside bore, the faces, and all notches used for seating.

Check the Output Shaft

Check the output shaft to make sure that it is running true because any changes affect the alignment of components and other operations within the transmission. Even being 0.001 inch out of round will throw corresponding components out of alignment, causing misdirection, wear, and even inoperability. These variances can come from normal wear. ■

7. C-springs: As these function, they act much like snap rings. Inspect them the same for flatness, cracks, and abrasions.
8. The third/fourth-gear synchronizer assembly (1 of 2): See the first bullet point in the "Synchronizers" section regarding synchronizer inspection.
9. Bronze blocker ring: Note that this is made from bronze. Thoroughly check all of the teeth, the inside bore, the faces, and all notches used for seating.
10. Third gear: Check all teeth for unusual wear, chips, and cracks. The wear pattern should be consistent and uniform across the teeth. Check the inside bore for abrasions. Check the gears for trueness.
11. Second gear: Check all teeth for unusual wear, chips, and cracks. The wear pattern should be consistent and uniform across the teeth. Check the inside bore for abrasions. Check the gears for trueness.
12. Bronze blocker ring: Note that this is made from bronze. Thoroughly check all of the teeth, the inside bore, the faces, and all notches used for seating.
13. C-spring: As these function similar to snap rings, inspect them the same way for flatness, bends, kinks, and abrasions.
14. First/second synchronizer assembly (2 of 2): See the first bullet point in the "Synchronizers" section regarding synchronizer inspection.
15. Bronze blocker ring: Note that this is made from bronze. Thoroughly check all of the teeth, the inside bore, the faces, and all notches used for seating.
16. First gear: Check all teeth for unusual wear, chips, and cracks. The wear pattern should be consistent and uniform across the teeth. Check the inside bore for abrasions. Check the gears for trueness.

Checklist #2

This next group of components on the output shaft consist of typically replaceable parts. From the front of the output shaft, the nine pieces are:

1. Snap ring (1 of 3 same size): Check for flatness, cracks, and chips.
2. Snap ring (1 only): Check for flatness, cracks, and chips.
3. Second-gear thrust washers (with tang): Check for flatness, galling, and wear.
4. Snap ring (1 only): Check for flatness, cracks, and chips.
5. Steel ball (for speedometer gear): Since these are encased in plastic, wear is usually not a problem on the ball as much as on the plastic gear.
6. First-gear thrust washer: Check for flatness, galling, and wear.
7. Rear bearing: Check ball bearings, inside and outside races, cage, and surfaces.
8. Snap ring (for rear bearing): Check for flatness, cracks, and chips.
9. Speedometer drive gear: Teeth should be even across without any dips in the teeth.

With all of the parts passing inspection, the next step is to incorporate the parts that are being replaced into the others that are being kept and used. Once you are sure that they will work together, assembly can begin.

Assembly

All of the new and old parts have now been cleaned, inspected, and laid out for assembly. At this point in the process, the builder should have a good idea of the sequence in which a Toploader is assembled. The better the builder knows the assembly sequence, the more comfortable and effective that he or she can be.

Do not be afraid to refer to the manual for the correct steps or to routinely double-check important assembly aspects. For example, 51 different parts need to be attached to the output shaft. That leaves plenty of opportunity to make an error, including missing the correct sequences or not installing the parts in their precise orientation. Consider reading (and maybe even studying) this chapter before beginning the final assembly.

Your starting point when rebuilding a Toploader may look similar to this. The trick is to assemble all of the parts in the best way possible. Using the best parts, the best assembly methods, and the best information produces the best results. (Photo Courtesy David Randal)

Predetermined Sequences

The order of some assembly sequences must be determined before the assembly begins. For example, do you want to assemble the synchronizers in advance or during the overall assembly? Assembling the synchronizers before the overall building sequence allows you to focus on them more to ensure that they are assembled correctly. In addition, assembling the synchronizers ahead of time will not take away from the rhythm and momentum of the overall assembly.

Another assembly sequence involves the two main bearings: the front and the rear. Generally, these bearings require the use of a press to remove/install them into their working position in the transmission. Under the "Inside the Case" heading in chapter 4, I mentioned some alternate procedures and to possibly avoid them for final assembly. The decision to use or not to use those methods must be made before the final assembly begins, as those methods involve some machining and massaging of the related parts. Either way, a builder is best served by researching and making the decisions on the bearings before the final assembly begins.

Needle Bearings

Another sequence involves positioning all of the needle bearings into their respective locations before beginning the final assembly. Three Toploader components require multiple sets of needle bearings. The input shaft uses 15, and the cluster gear uses a total of 42 for both ends of that gear. Finally, the reverse-gear assembly uses a total of 44 needle bearings for its two ends.

Most experienced builders use an oil-soluble product, such as a light assembly lube or petroleum jelly, to keep the bearings in place during assembly. Therefore, it may be easier to assemble the needle-bearing components together as a group. Similar to the reasons for preassembling the synchronizers, having components ready to install maintains rhythm and momentum during the final assembly.

An advantage to building these assemblies ahead of time is not having 10 bearings rolling around and not having to keep track of them on a busy workbench. A smaller factor is having to stop to remove the above-mentioned lube or jelly from your hands.

The three sets of needle bearings are all different from each other. The longest ones are for the cluster gear (two sets of 21 each). The shortest ones are for the input shaft (one set of 15). Those that are sized in between the others in length go into the reverse cluster gear (two sets of 22).

Plan to research and make the decisions for or against these operations before the final assembly.

Assembly

The only items remaining are some preassembly preparation and last-minute assembly tips. These seven tips can make things go more smoothly when assembling a Toploader. Keep the following information in mind when you lay out the parts for assembly as well as when you install them.

Orientation is important in any build. Know the correct orientation of every part and install each one in that manner. Double-checking is wise. If a mistake was made while the transmission was being assembled, the transmission will need to be removed from the vehicle, and the build must start over. Of course, starting over costs time and money to pay for new consumables and to replace any damaged parts. In addition, installing parts incorrectly may damage other parts, and you may need to replace some of the more expensive parts. The goal is to build one Toploader and build it correctly.

When installing synchronizer strut keys (also called dogs) the longer keys are for the first/second-gear synchronizer assembly. All first/second-gear keys (both old and new) have a notch on one end for quick identification. The direction of the notch when the keys are installed is important. They should be installed with the notch toward the rear of the transmission. The inner and outer synchronizer hubs can only go together one way to operate correctly, allowing the transmission to be completely assembled and work properly.

During the inspection phase, the shift rails should have received a thorough check. Make sure that each part of the shift-rail assembly is in the correct place and that it operates. Shift rails come in sets, and Ford used six different types of shift-rail sets during the run of the Toploader. Most use all the same size and shape of detents throughout the assembly for their model year. The first design used round-headed detents in some locations and hatchet-headed detents in others. A total of five different sizes and shapes of detents include round head, hatchet head, short blunt, short pointed, and long pointed.

The synchronizer keys (left) have two sizes that are dedicated to the synchronizer with which they work. The shorter keys (top left) go into the third/fourth-gear synchronizer. The longer keys (bottom left) fit the first/second-gear synchronizer. This photo also shows the different bore sizes of the gears. (Photo Courtesy David Randal)

Complete rail and detent information is in chapter 2.

If you are satisfied that all rails are ready to be installed, look at where they will be positioned in the case. If an original case is used, make sure that there is no damage to the shift-rail beds before installation. If using a new case, make sure that they fit and operate correctly in their new home. In addition, check their condition for damage, burrs, and anything else that could impede smooth and correct operation.

If the Toploader to be rebuilt is 1968 or newer, the first/second-gear detent bore will not have a set screw for the top detent spring. Instead, Ford used a longer spring that relies on the cover holding it in place when it is torqued in its proper position. During assembly, a small, flat piece of metal and one of the nearby holes and cover bolts can be used to act as a temporary hold-down. This also applies pressure so that the first/second-gear detent and spring will be in their proper working positions for bench testing with the cover removed.

Preassemble compound-parts assemblies, such as synchronizers, ahead of the final assembly. Try to avoid rabbit holes that take your thoughts and momentum away from focusing solely on the correct sequence of the final assembly. Building those items ahead of time will keep a build progressing, having just to install the assemblies and check their positioning. Then, continue with the final assembly.

Assembly lube is almost always used during the assembly phase of most machines. In the case of a Toploader transmission, using these lubes is not always a good idea. Unlike an engine that has an oil pump, an OEM Toploader never had a lubricant pump and creates very little lubrication pressure. Instead, the lubricant delivery system of a Toploader uses small oil passages and grooves. Lubrication is delivered via the gears dipping into the pool of lubricant at the bottom of the case and the kinetic motion of its parts. The lubricant moves into smaller, harder-to-reach areas via small holes, grooves, and passages, where it keeps critical components properly oiled.

Some assembly lubes do not break down fast enough and can clog the small passages and grooves during initial use, causing severe damage. When needing a grease-like product that can hold parts, such as needle bearings, in place during assembly, a good substitute is petroleum jelly. This is not to be confused with the light coatings of oil on the components to have them pre-lubricated upon testing, break-in, and the first running.

Synchronizer Tips

Both inner synchronizer hubs have a wide and narrow face at the main shaft splines. The wide machined face on the first/second-gear synchronizer faces toward the rear of the transmission and provides the thrust surface for the front of first gear. The narrow face faces toward the front of the transmission and has a snap ring placed in front of it. The wide machined face on the third/fourth-gear synchronizer also faces toward the rear of the transmission and provides the thrust surface for the front of third gear. The narrow face goes toward the front of the transmission with a snap ring placed in front of it as well.

The synchronizer's inner hubs have two different-size splined holes through the center. The one with the larger hole is for the first/second-gear synchronizer, and the one with the smaller hole is for the third/fourth-gear synchronizer.

The outer hub on the third/fourth-gear synchronizer has a side with more machined steps on it. This side needs to face the front of the transmission for assembly.

The first/second-gear synchronizer outer ring has a distinctive straight-cut-tooth gear around its outside diameter. When fully assembled and in its finished location, position it between the first and second gears.

The first/second-gear synchronizer's shifter-fork groove should be mounted toward the rear of the case.

When orienting the inner and outer hubs of a synchronizer, there are three keys (or dogs) to be installed. Load a C-spring on each side. There is one hump on the center of each C-spring, and that needs to go to the same dog on both sides. Make sure to not stagger the humps on the C-springs from side to side. They need to be in the same key on each side of the synchronizer hub. Otherwise, they will pop out during use. More details on the synchronizer assembly are in the "Synchronizer Assemblies" section in this chapter.

Shift-Rail Tips

It is much easier to check the shift rails in advance than to check them after they have been installed—and it takes more work to correct. In addition, understanding how they work can help you assemble them correctly.

Shift rails work in unison. Moving one rail will raise the interlock pins that keep other rails from moving. This lock-out action keeps the transmission from engaging two gears at the same time. Some builders prefer laying them all out in position and pre-fitting the rail systems to ensure that they will be installed in their correct locations. Doing this also helps a builder understand how they work in unison.

A shortcut for installing detents and pins is to use a long, flat-head screwdriver with a ground-down tip. This tool also comes in handy during other stages of assembly. David Kee uses a piece of 3/16-inch brake line with a flare on one end to install his detents. Hold the detent by its side with a telescoping magnet and line the detent up over the hole in which it goes. Then, push the detent into place with the brake line and remove the magnet.

Any time you handle a shift rail, check whether the rail needs any deburring to operate smoothly and without any drag through the bores that it will occupy.

Shift-Rail Installation Order

When installing shift rails for the forward gears, the third/fourth-gear shift rail needs to be installed before the first/second-gear shift rail. This is more about easier access than anything else.

On the first/second- and third/fourth-gear shift rails and on the side of the rail with three notches, you may find a raised area on the square end of the front and rear notches. This is from the detent stopping the travel of the rail during shifts. This same condition may also exist on the reverse rail on the side with two notches. These can be dressed down to keep the rail from dragging in the bores of the case.

Shift rails fall into the same category as cams, shafts, and output shafts in that they can be polished and checked for accuracy and runout on a lathe. Polishing is a step that many builders also include to reduce friction and increase the ease of operation.

Sequence Order	Part
1	Reverse detent spring
2	Reverse detent
3	Reverse shift rail
4	Reverse interlock detent
5	Third/fourth-gear shift rail with interlock pin
6	Third/fourth-gear detent from the driver's side of the case
7	Third/fourth-gear detent spring
8	Third/fourth-gear detent bolt
9	Back on top of the third/fourth-gear shift-rail interlock detent
10	First/second-gear shift-rail
11	First/second-gear shift-rail detent
12	First/second-gear shift-rail detent spring
13	First/second-gear detent set screw if used

Shift rails work in conjunction with their detents. It helps to know which detents work with which shift rails. With the various shapes and sizes of detents that Toploaders use, knowing which ones go where is critical for proper assembly.

All shift rails use a shift fork for shifting. As such, the two pieces must be installed in conjunction with each other. As the shift rail is being inserted into its bosses in the case, the shift fork must be "slid" onto the shift rail as the rail goes into position. Sometimes, this also includes the installation of a detent and a detent spring. There is a sequential order to these procedures, and sometimes, the shift rail is used to hold a detent in place.

The correct sequence for installing all shift rails and detents is listed in the table above.

By now, a builder should be familiar with all of the parts and how the assemblies go together. An inventory list is good to use to check off the progressive steps. Toploaders are assembled similar to how they are disassembled—that is, they follow a sequence and order. Familiarize yourself with this sequence and concentrate on not missing or changing any steps.

The Building Sequence

Now that every part has been thoroughly inspected and the necessary parts have been replaced, it's time to reassemble the Toploader. Use a large, flat, and clean work surface to lay out all of the parts and assemblies. Laying out the parts on a clean surface can help keep parts from moving out of position or getting mixed together. Make sure that the workspace is well lit. Assembly directions begin with a cleaned case being positioned with the opening on the top.

An overview of assembling a Toploader deals with the bottom shafts of reverse and the cluster gear. Next, install the fully loaded output shaft with its two bearings. The shifting and detent components follow before attaching the tailhousing and external components. The building sequence is essentially the reverse of disassembly.

It's important to get lubricant well into the bores for the shifter cam and levers from the inside of the case. The idea is to prevent the rubber O-ring from positioning itself into a dry hole. Just like the rubber gasket on an oil filter, that little bit of oil keeps the O-ring from leaking. (Photo Courtesy David Randal)

Liberally lube the shafts, O-rings, and case bores for the shifter cam and levers before installing them to begin the assembly process. The O-rings must fit the grooves without any twisting and seat in that groove freely. (Photo Courtesy David Randal)

Install the shifter cams and levers by lubricating the O-rings, shafts, and case bores liberally before firmly pushing the shifter cams into the holes on the driver's side of the main case. Note the size of these pieces. The three pieces consist of two that are the same for the forward gears and one that is different for reverse. The longer cam/shaft is for the reverse gear and goes into the center hole with the flat portion and pinpointing down. The two shorter ones are first/second gear and third/fourth gear, and they go into the front and rear holes with the flat portion and pinpointing up. The two shorter ones are interchangeable with each other.

Check that the O-rings are properly oiled and seated correctly on the shafts. There should be no binds or twists so that they seal and work properly.

If it has not already been done during preassembly, coat the two bores inside the cluster gear with a light, oil-soluble grease or petroleum jelly and install the 21 needle bearings

The shifter cams and shafts are two different sizes and need to go into the correct bores to operate properly. The shorter ones are for first/second or third/fourth, they can interchange, and they can be installed facing upward. The shorter one is used for reverse only and should go into the middle of the three holes, facing down. (Photo Courtesy David Randal)

When properly lubed and installed into the case, the shifter cams and levers should look like this. The two that are facing up are for the first/second and third/fourth gears. The one that is facing down is for the reverse gear. Note the difference of the reverse cam/lever. (Photo Courtesy David Randal)

in each end. The needle-bearing retainers go on the outside of the needle-bearing bore next to the thrust washer. A piece of 9-inch long, 1/2-inch polyvinyl-chloride (PVC) pipe can be used as a dummy shaft in the cluster gear to keep the needle bearings in place during assembly. This PVC pipe will be removed later during assembly.

Inside the main case, coat the machined cluster-gear thrust surfaces with a thin film of lubricant and position the lubricated thrust washers on both ends of the case.

Position the cluster gear, dummy shaft, thrust bearings, roller bearings, and roller retainer in the case. This is a temporary position. The assembled cluster gear should be located as low as possible for clearance to install other components.

The idea is to place the cluster gear now, as opposed to later, when

The cluster gear is shown with its needle bearings and their retainer installed. Note the lube holding the needle bearings in place for installing the cluster gear. Needle bearings and retainers must be installed on both ends of the cluster gear. (Photo Courtesy David Randal)

Note the alignment of the small tab on the thrust washer for the cluster gear. At this point, the cluster gear is being placed close to its finished position and will be finally located later in the build. The thrust washers cannot be installed later in the build when the cluster gear is installed permanently, so install them now. (Photo Courtesy David Randal)

Installing the cluster gear's two thrust washers is easier when placing them in the cluster-gear bed instead of trying to keep them attached to the gear itself during installation. Use lubricant to hold them in place. (Photo Courtesy David Randal)

When assembling the parts for the cluster gear, it's easier to position the thrust washers in the cluster-gear bed with a thin film of lubricant or petroleum jelly to hold them in place. Note the proximity of the reverse idler-gear bed. Some builders install the reverse idler gear before the cluster gear. It makes no difference either way because both need to be in place before the input and output shafts are installed.

As with the assembly of the reverse idler gear, the needle bearings installed in both ends must have their bearing retainers put in place. The retainers hold the needle bearings and the lubricant and/or assembly grease in place within the cluster gear. (Photo Courtesy David Randal)

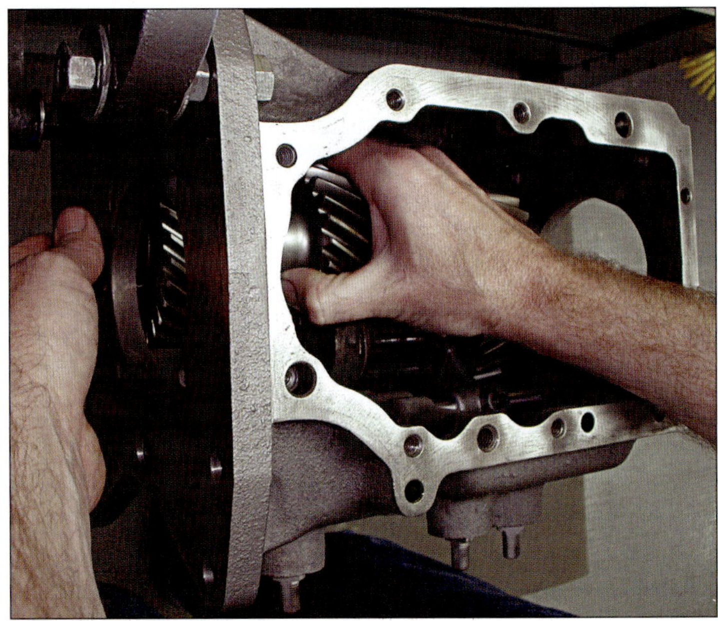

Place the cluster gear with its needle bearings and retainers into its position. For now, the cluster gear will lay on the bottom of the case so that there is clearance for other components during the assembly. (Photo Courtesy David Randal)

The cluster gear being in its temporary position with the dummy shaft in place is almost exactly the same as the finished position. The cluster gear will be placed in its final position later in the build process. (Photo Courtesy David Randal)

When preparing to install the reverse idler gear, there are 44 needle bearings, 2 thrust washers, and 2 needle-bearing retainers that make up that assembly. The needle bearings, retainers, and thrust washers are non-directional and can work on either side. (Photo Courtesy David Randal)

it will not fit in the case with the fully assembled output shaft in place. The cluster gear will not rest in its finished position until later in the build. It is in a temporary position and will be moved later to engage with the upper geartrain for its final positioning.

Place the case in a vertical position with the front of the case facing down. The bore for the cluster-gear shaft needs clearance for removal of the temporary shaft during this step. Align the bore of the cluster gear and the thrust washers with the bores in the case and install the cluster-gear shaft from the back of the case. Use the cluster-gear shaft to push the temporary PVC pipe out of the cluster gear and through the cluster-gear bore in the front of the case.

Return the case to the previous horizontal position with the opening facing up. Check the cluster-gear endplay with a feeler gauge. The factory specification for endplay is 0.004 to 0.018 inch. If it is not within these specifications, replace the thrust washers.

After establishing the correct endplay, remove the cluster-gear shaft while reinstalling the dummy shaft in its place and allow the gear to remain sitting at the bottom of the case. Checking cluster-gear endplay at this stage is easier without other components limiting access. The dummy shaft is used to temporarily replace the cluster-gear shaft during removal and holds the needle bearings in place during assembly. The dummy shaft will be removed later in the build.

Much like the cluster gear, coat the two end bores in the reverse idler-gear shaft with a light, oil-soluble grease or petroleum jelly (if this was not already done during preassembly). Install the 22 needle bearings in each end. Place the needle-bearing retainers on the

There are 22 needle bearings that go into each end of the reverse idler gear. Install them using oil-soluble grease or petroleum jelly to hold them in place and cap each end with its needle-bearing retainer. (Photo Courtesy David Randal)

The bearing retainer caps the needle bearings on the reverse idler-gear assembly. It fits into the reverse idler gear and keeps the bearings trapped in position. This needs to be done on both ends of the reverse idler gear. (Photo Courtesy David Randal)

Applying assembly grease or lubricant to the two reverse idler-gear thrust washers requires lubricant on both sides for the best results. It's easier to lubricate the thrust washers before they are installed into their respective locations and exposure is physically limited. (Photo Courtesy David Randal)

A thrust washer goes on each end of the reverse idler gear. Lubricate them and the gear's bed prior to installing them in their bed in the case. The lubrication will help to keep them in place. (Photo Courtesy David Randal)

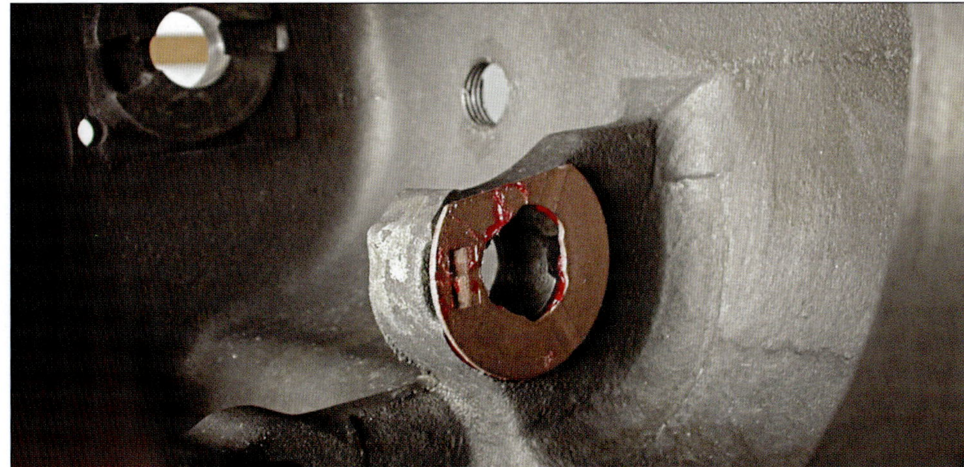

This is the correct orientation for the metallic thrust washers that go on each end of the reverse idler gear. Since there is a relief cut into the washers to fit the case, they can only fit one way into the reverse idler-gear bed. (Photo Courtesy David Randal)

When fully installed, the reverse idler gear looks like this. Note the difference between the two styles of gears (helical and straight cut). The straight-cut gear engages with another similar gear on the outside of the first/second-gear synchronizer.

outside of the needle bearings next to the thrust washer.

Coat the machined reverse idler-gear thrust surfaces in the case with a thin film of lubricant. Then, position the two lubricated thrust washers in place.

The reverse spur gear is the one with the reverse splines. Install it with the straight-cut gear toward the helical-cut gear. Position the reverse shift-fork groove facing toward the front of the transmission.

Position the reverse idler gear, the sliding gear, and the roller (needle) bearings in place, making sure that the shift-fork groove of the sliding gear is still facing toward the front of the case. Align the reverse-gear bore and thrust washers with the case bores and install the reverse idler shaft. Insert the reverse idler-gear shaft with the roll pin lining up with the recess in the outside of the case.

If you are installing the roll pin for the first time, insert the roll pin into the shaft with it sticking out one side. There is a notch in the case near the hole that holds the roll pin and shaft in place in its final position.

Installing the reverse shift rail

Install the reverse idler gear with the helical gear toward the rear of the case. Line up the gear, the two needle-bearing retainers, and the two thrust washers to receive the reverse-idler-gear shaft from the rear of the case. (Photo Courtesy David Randal)

The next detent component is the detent plug that is positioned on top of the spring in the reverse detent hole. It will need to be pushed down to install the reverse shifter rail. A ground-down screwdriver or a piece of brake line can be used for this.

involves doing a few steps at the same time but still in a sequence. The shift rail, detent, detent spring, and reverse shift fork need to be installed in conjunction with each other. Use the steps to accomplish this correctly.

Lubricate the shift-rail bore and the slot that the shift cam engages on the reverse shift fork. Set the reverse shift fork in the reverse idler-gear-fork slot and against the reverse cam and

The spring for the reverse detent components is the first to go in the detent hole in the cover face. Note the three bosses (below where the spring is being inserted) that hold all three of the shift rails in working alignment. (Photo Courtesy David Randal)

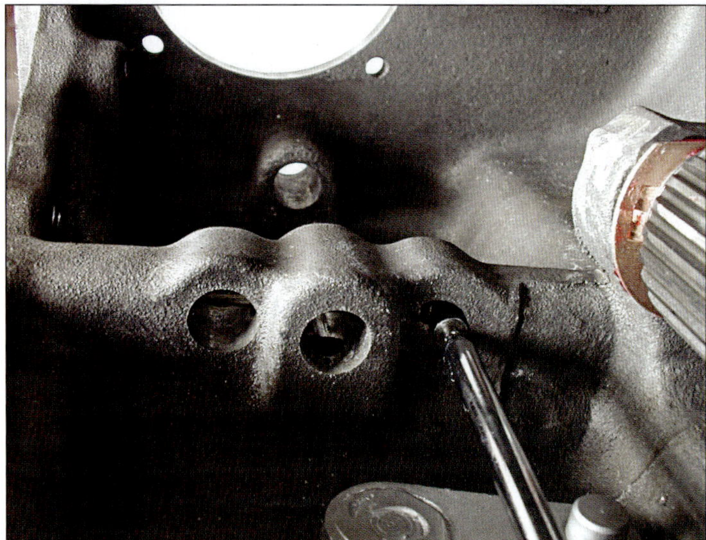

Insert the reverse detent into its position after the reverse detent spring has been installed. These two pieces must be installed before the reverse shift rail goes all the way into place. A magnet is used here to position it correctly. (Photo Courtesy David Randal)

This view shows the three bores of the shift rails (upper left). Also shown is the piece of brake line that is holding down the reverse detent plug and the spring used for compressing the spring and plug for the installation of the reverse shifter rail. (Photo Courtesy David Randal)

Position the reverse shift fork in its operating position onto the reverse-idler-gear assembly for lining up with its shift rail. Lube the contact areas between the shift fork and the reverse gear's slot where the fork will ride. (Photo Courtesy David Randal)

Oil the reverse shift rail and insert it into the reverse-shift-rail bores and through the reverse shift fork. Work it in the center shift-rail boss until it reaches the detent, making sure that it seats the shift fork without any wedging that would change the alignment with the reverse gear's shift-fork slot. (Photo Courtesy David Randal)

With the shift fork in its proper working position and alignment on the reverse-idler-gear assembly, continue moving the reverse shift rail toward the center of the case and into its last casting boss. The shift rail needs only to reach the end of the boss to align its detent. (Photo Courtesy David Randal)

The reverse shift rail will go into the case's rail bores only to the first detent notch. A this point, the set screw can be installed, and reverse will be in the neutral position. (Photo Courtesy David Randal)

After installing the reverse-gear shift-rail detent spring and detent plug, the reverse shift rail and shifter fork can be installed. Make sure that all components are in their proper positions before securing the set screw in the shifter fork. (Photo Courtesy David Randal)

The reverse-idler-gear assembly, the shift fork being engaged in its slot, and the reverse shift rail are shown all in perfect alignment with the shift-fork set screw installed. Again, note the proximity of the cam and levers in the rear, as they control the movement of the shift rails. (Photo Courtesy David Randal)

shaft pin. Lubricate the shift-rail bosses in the case and install the reverse shift rail from the rear of the case with the side of the rail having two notches facing down in the case.

Compress the detent spring by pushing down on the reverse detent and pushing forward on the reverse shift rail at the same time. Use a tool such as a piece of brake line to hold down the detent and its spring. The rail will pass over the detent and stop against the tool that is pressing down. Next, holding a light forward pressure on the reverse shift rail, remove the tool and the rail will move forward until the detent engages the first notch in the rail. The reverse shift rail does not go all the way inside at this point.

Insert the reverse-gear shift rail the rest of the way inside. This is the last time to check for any drag points on the reverse shift rail. It's not too late to polish any drag points, as they will be inaccessible from this point forward. The reverse shift rail goes through the reverse shift fork and into the center shift-rail boss in the case to the first of two notches.

After you are sure of the proper placement of the detents, shift rail, and shift fork, install the set screw into the reverse shifter fork and tighten it.

Install the detent that goes between the reverse rail and the third/fourth-gear shift rail with the reverse rail pushed toward the rear of the case. The detent should drop completely into the bore and will allow the third/fourth-gear shift rail to pass in a later step.

If the detent does not go all the way down, make sure that the reverse shift rail is in the neutral position by pushing it as far back as it will go by hand or by rotating the reverse cam and shaft counterclockwise.

Sequence 1

This is the first of several sequence points during the assembly. At this step of that process, the focus shifts from the case to the output shaft. The components on the output shaft will be assembled, and the sequence and orientation in which they are assembled are important. If you are not sure of both when assembling the output shaft, double-check the procedures. The idea is to "load" the output shaft with its gears, synchronizers, bearings, snap rings, and washers the correct way, working from the back of the output shaft to the front.

Synchronizer Assemblies

A builder has the choice to assemble the synchronizers ahead of time or in this sequence. Most builders prefer doing it ahead of the final assembly. The two synchronizers in a Toploader require special attention, as they are the most complicated assemblies within the transmission and contain potential installation problems.

Keep in mind that when both are assembled, the two synchronizers will not be identical—nor will they be interchangeable. The biggest difference is two different internal spline dimensions for positioning on the output shaft. Another difference is that the first/second-gear synchronizer has a straight-cut gear on the outside of it that is used for reverse. The third/fourth-gear synchronizer does not have any gears on its circumference. There are three synchronizer key (or dog) inserts, one inner hub, two C-springs, and an outer sleeve to each assembled synchronizer.

A Toploader uses four identical bronze blocker rings. They are used for the first, second, and third gears and are located on the input shaft, fitting the mating side of the two synchronizers. While the blocker rings interact with the synchronizers, they are typically assembled with the gears.

The synchronizer's two inner hubs' splines match the two on the output shaft to complete the connection to the gears. The two output-shaft splines are different from each other and are dedicated to the first/second- and third/fourth-gear synchronizers.

Check the fitment and operation of both synchronizer sets' components. If it makes it easier for assembly, separate the two sets and build them separately.

Just because parts may be new, there is no guarantee that they will fit perfectly. This statement is true about synchronizers. Each part should be test fit with its mating parts (new or old). Test fit the mating parts with each other and then test fit the finished assembly as a whole unit.

Watch for any synchronizer parts that don't seat correctly with each other as they are assembled. If they seat too deep or too shallow, the poor fitment will cause problems that will require another disassembly.

Check the spline gear and its keys for fitment with the new synchronizer ring as well.

Remember that the dogs are dedicated for each of the two synchronizers, with the shorter ones going on the third/fourth-gear synchronizer. The C-springs locate with and away from the dogs.

Install the synchronizer keys and C-springs in the synchronizer assemblies. The longer keys with the notch at one end go in the first/second-gear synchronizer.

Locate the hump in the C-springs in the same dog on both sides.

Assembling the Synchronizers

1 *A fully assembled Toploader synchronizer is used for first/second gear and is recognizable by the straight-cut gears on the outside of the assembly. Note the three dogs and how their position relates to the C-spring and inner hub. (Photo Courtesy David Randal)*

2 The main components of the two synchronizers are shown, and the two C-springs are on top. The synchronizer on the left is for third/fourth gear. The synchronizer on the right is from first/second gear. The bottom row has the synchronizer keys, or dogs. Note the differences in the internal diameters that fit the output shaft and the sizes of the keys. (Photo Courtesy David Randal)

3 When installing the keys, or dogs, make sure that the correct dog is being used for that specific synchronizer. The dogs slide into the opening between the inner and outer hubs after they have been lined up. The first/second-gear synchronizer, which uses the longer dogs, is shown. (Photo Courtesy David Randal)

4 After matching the correct inner and outer hubs of the first/second-gear synchronizer, inserting the C-spring begins by positioning the end of the C-spring against one of the three dogs. Then, line it up to meet the second dog before clipping the other end onto the third dog. (Photo Courtesy David Randal)

5 There are three dogs in each synchronizer. The correct way to install a dog into a synchronizer is with the opening toward the center. The opening provides a place for the C-springs to ride and lock in. (Photo Courtesy David Randal)

6 *The synchronizer's C-springs are mounted inside the synchronizer and hold the inner and outer pieces together. There is only one C-spring per synchronizer. The C-spring must ride in all three dogs when properly installed into their synchronizers. (Photo Courtesy David Randal)*

Output-Shaft Assemblies

Now, the sequence of installing parts onto the output shaft begins. It starts from the bottom (driveshaft) end of the output shaft, and the builder works up to the top (front) end of the output shaft. Parts are locked in place with snap rings and washer/spacers to hold their positions.

Install the first/second-gear synchronizer onto the front of the output shaft, sliding it partially down the shaft. Make sure that the shift-fork groove is facing down (toward the rear of the shaft). The longer keys with the notch at one end go in the first/second-gear synchronizer with the notch in the keys facing the rear of the case.

As this begins the output-shaft assembly, note that the wrong type of grease or assembly lube could block the small oil passages in the oiling system.

A snap ring is mounted onto the output shaft after the first/second-gear synchronizer and holds it in position.

All four blocker rings are the same and can be mixed in their positioning within the two synchronizers. (See the "Synchronizer Assemblies" section earlier in this chapter.) Make sure that the blocker rings face the correct direction with the synchronizers and engage properly. Position the first blocker ring onto second gear.

Lubricate the bore of the gear, the outside cone, and the output shaft with gear or light assembly oil. Slide second gear and its blocker ring onto the front of the output shaft, making sure that the inserts in the synchronizer engage with the notches in the blocker ring.

In this order, install second gear, the tanged thrust washer, and its accompanying snap ring onto the output shaft. Make sure that the tanged washer is in its correct position and that the snap ring is squarely in its groove for both to be seated properly.

Place the second blocker ring on third gear. Make sure that they engage easily and properly.

Lubricate the bore of third gear and the output shaft with gear or assembly oil. Slide third gear and the blocker ring onto the output shaft with the blocker ring toward the front of the shaft.

Slide the third/fourth-gear synchronizer onto the output shaft, making sure that the inserts in the synchronizer engage the notches in the blocker ring.

Install the snap ring on the front of the output shaft to hold the third/fourth-gear synchronizer in place. Slide the outside hub of the third/fourth-gear synchronizer over third gear so that the output shaft assembly can clear the front of the case opening during installation.

At this point, the process switches from working from the front (top) of the output shaft to the rear (bottom). Correctly position the third blocker ring onto first gear.

Lubricate the bore of the gear and output shaft with gear or assembly oil. Slide first gear and its blocker ring onto the rear of the output shaft, making sure that the notches in the blocker ring engage the synchronizer inserts. It should be positioned on the other side of the first/second-gear synchronizer.

Install the heavy thrust washer that goes on the rear or bottom of the output shaft. Make sure that it is fully lubricated.

Assembling Components onto the Output Shaft

1 *The first assembly to be installed onto the output shaft is the first/second-gear synchronizer. It goes on from the front, and the shift-fork groove needs to face the rear of the output shaft. Always take care to not scratch or mar the surface of the output shaft. (Photo Courtesy David Randal)*

2 *The snap ring must be installed to lock the first/second-gear synchronizer onto the output shaft. This snap ring is installed on the front side of the synchronizer. A step on the output shaft keeps the synchronizer from moving rearward on the output shaft. (Photo Courtesy David Randal)*

3 *Many builders get into the habit of applying a fresh coat of oil to the output shaft as parts and assemblies are attached. This step puts lubrication in place for the initial start-up of the transmission and helps reduce and prevent scoring. (Photo Courtesy David Randal)*

4 *Builders can lubricate each component (inside and out) for protection before they are installed onto the output shaft. The idea is to have lubricant where it is needed when the transmission is put into gear for the first time. (Photo Courtesy David Randal)*

5 *When oiling the parts for assembly, include the cones (both inside and out). These critical areas are among the higher friction surfaces of the transmission and need that initial lubricant upon the first start-up. Another trick is to use an oil squirt gun after the gear is located onto the output shaft. (Photo Courtesy David Randal)*

6 *Add the blocker ring (note the correct direction) to the step of second gear before installing them onto the output shaft. The four blocker rings are identical, but their placement and orientation are critical to the build. (Photo Courtesy David Randal)*

7 *Install second gear onto the output shaft, making sure to mate it to the first/second-gear synchronizer correctly. In this order, install second gear, the tanged thrust washer, and its accompanying snap ring onto the output shaft. (Photo Courtesy David Randal)*

8 After installing second gear and its blocker ring onto the output shaft from the front, check the fitment of that blocker ring with the synchronizer and its engagement gears. Ensure correct positioning of the first/second-gear synchronizer and second gear.

9 Brush oil into the grooves for the thrust washer and snap ring. Every surface on the output shaft and its components needs lubrication for operation. Adding oil during assembly puts lubrication into these critical areas for initial start-up. (Photo Courtesy David Randal)

10 The tanged thrust washer needs to be positioned correctly for proper fitment. The tang in the inside diameter of the washer needs to match up with the groove in the output shaft. (Photo Courtesy David Randal)

11 To be seated correctly, the tanged thrust washer must be installed by positioning the tang in its groove. Then, work the washer down into its groove in the output shaft until it is finally seated. Check that it is not locked into an incorrect position. (Photo Courtesy David Randal)

12 *Using the groove on the output shaft, install the snap ring, making sure that it is seated properly and can slide around within that groove. The thrust washer rides on the same output-shaft outside diameter just above second gear. With the two pieces installed, look for any excess slop in their fitment. (Photo Courtesy David Randal)*

14 *Again, oil the output shaft as assembly progresses. Oil the area where third gear will be added to the output shaft (next to second gear). Install third gear, oiling the bore on the gearsets as well to ensure good protection. (Photo Courtesy David Randal)*

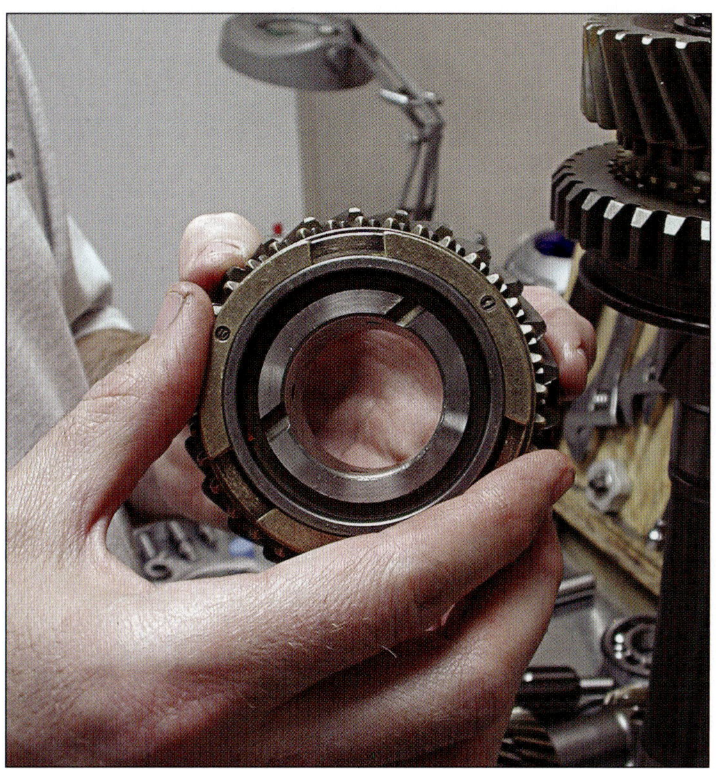

13 *Fit the blocker ring to the correct side of third gear, making sure that it fits over the cone on the gear. Oiling the output shaft and cone as pieces are added is a good way to keep oil on surfaces that need protection for initial start-up. (Photo Courtesy David Randal)*

15 *Install the third/fourth-gear synchronizer onto the output shaft. The synchronizer should slide onto the output shaft with minimal side-to-side movement to seat it. Make sure that the inserts in the synchronizer engage the notches in the blocker ring to fully engage the pair. (Photo Courtesy David Randal)*

16 *With third gear securely installed, add the third/fourth-gear synchronizer to the output shaft. The face of the synchronizer with more machined grooves should be facing upward (toward the front of the case). Lock the synchronizer into place by installing its snap ring. (Photo Courtesy David Randal)*

17 *After adding a liberal amount of lubricant to the output shaft, cone, and the inner bore of the gearset, add a blocker ring to first gear from the rear of the output shaft. Make sure to line up the teeth of the blocker ring with the engagement-gear teeth of first gear. (Photo Courtesy David Randal)*

18 *Prior to installing first gear onto the output shaft, oil the shaft's surface liberally. Pre-lubing every component and assembly helps keep a level of lubricant on surfaces for initial start-up to protect those surfaces. Once the transmission is engaged, the oiling system will move the lubricant throughout the transmission. (Photo Courtesy David Randal)*

19 *With plenty of lubrication on the mating surfaces, add the larger steel thrust washer on top of first gear. This is the last step on the bench for output-shaft assembly before it is installed into the case. Double-check the positioning of all of the components one last time. (Photo Courtesy David Randal)*

Output-Shaft Installation

Introducing the output shaft and its newly fitted components into the case is the next step. It will take a bit of juggling, as the output shaft is longer than the case, and that can affect balancing all of the components on that shaft. Using two hands for this process is the only way to accomplish this. One hand can hold first gear and the thrust washer in place on the output shaft while the other should be farther up the output shaft to control its movement into the case.

Support the thrust washer and first gear against the first/second-gear synchronizer to prevent them from sliding off the shaft. Then, carefully lower the now-assembled output-shaft assembly into the case. Begin with the back end first, with the longer portion of the output shaft sticking out the hole in the back of the case.

Keep first gear in its correct position with your fingers while installing the output shaft fully into the case. The best method is to come straight down into the case with the driveshaft end of the output shaft. Then, change the angle of the output shaft to "lay down" the output shaft into its proper position and move the driveshaft end out the back of the case.

Installing the Output Shaft

1 The most effective way to introduce the assembled output shaft into the case is with two movements. For the first movement, aim the long side of the output shaft vertically into the case and then angle it out the hole on the back wall of the case. (Photo Courtesy David Randal)

2 For the second movement, with the output shaft exiting the hole in the back of the case, reduce the angle to make the output shaft and case parallel with each other. Then, lower the front of the output shaft into place within the case. (Photo Courtesy David Randal)

3 With the output shaft and all of its components in the case, this is the result. At this point, the forward-gear shift forks and shift rails are not installed. The rear main bearing has yet to be installed as well. (Photo Courtesy David Randal)

There are two methods to keep first gear in place when installing the output shaft into the case. One method is to physically hold the gear in place as the shaft goes into the case. Another method is to apply a temporary hose clamp to hold it and the washer in place during installation. Remember to remove the clamp once the output shaft is locked in with the input shaft.

TECH TIP

Shift Fork Differentiation

The two shift forks that are used for the forward gears are not interchangeable and must be installed in their correct locations. Luckily, there are easy ways to differentiate them.

The set-screw hole on the third/fourth-gear shift fork is recessed, whereas the one on the first/second-gear shift fork is not. In addition, the third/fourth-gear shift fork has more material around the shift-rail bore and has a longer slot where the shift-lever cam engages it. ■

Place the two shift forks into their respective positions, making sure that the correct shift fork is in the correct location. Shift forks are not interchangeable but can be easily identified. (Photo Courtesy David Randal)

Sequence 2

At this point, the shift forks and shift-rail alignment installations are nearly impossible to finalize, as the output shaft is not in place with the rear bearing installed. This can be frustrating to an inexperienced builder. Builders who rebuild numerous Toploaders often use a dummy bearing to hold the output shaft in place until the first/second and third/fourth shift rails are fully installed.

Use a small amount of petroleum jelly to hold the third/fourth-gear shift-rail interlock pin in place in the third/fourth-gear shift rail.

From the front of the case, begin to install the third/fourth-gear shift rail. Make sure that the side of the rail with three notches is facing the outside (driver's side) of the case. The set-screw hole should be in the "up" position for the third/fourth-gear shift fork. This will align the shift fork on the shift rail. Install only far enough to "thread" the shift rail through the shift fork. Lubricate the boss in which the shift rail will reside.

Position the third/fourth-gear shift fork in place on the third/fourth-gear synchronizer. Lubricate the shift-rail bore, the rail bosses in the case, and the slot that the shift cam engages on the third/fourth-gear shift fork. The set-screw hole will be facing upward, and the notches will be facing the driver's side of the transmission.

As the third/fourth-gear shift rail is being installed into its center shift-rail boss, watch for the set-screw hole in the shift rail to line up with the set-screw hole in the shift fork.

There is no adjustment. After the hole in the fork and the hole in

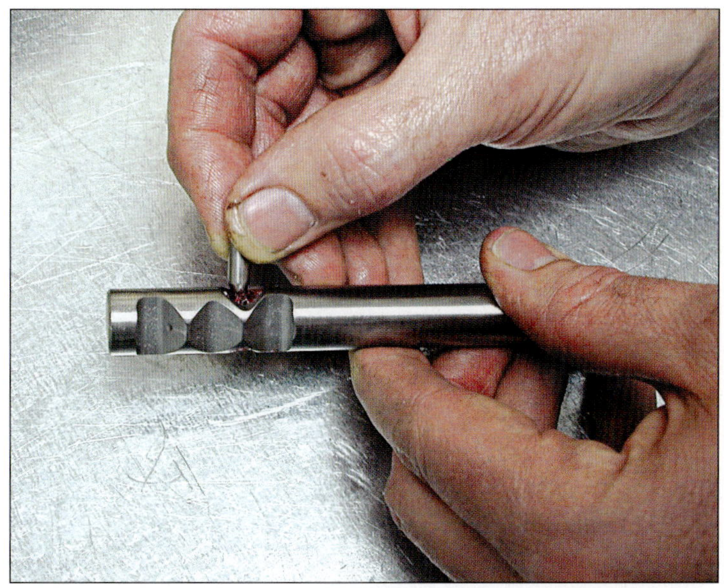

Apply a small dab of petroleum jelly into the hole for the third/fourth-gear shift-rail interlock and insert the interlock. There are three reliefs cut into the third/fourth-gear shift rail. With the interlock secured into the shift rail, insert the third/fourth-gear shift rail into the case from the front. Note the proximity of the cam and the lever on the driver's side of the case. (Photo Courtesy David Randal)

As the third/fourth-gear shift rail is being inserted into the boss in the case, it needs to "thread" through the third/fourth-gear shift fork. Keep the shift rail in the same position so that you do not disturb the interlock that has already been inserted into the third/fourth shift rail. (Photo Courtesy David Randal)

Polishing (or even grinding, if necessary) the high spots on shift rails during assembly is not unusual, and doing so will contribute to smoother shifting. Clean any parts that have been polished or ground and keep any grindings from entering the case or contacting other components. Another tip is to tighten the set screws. Some set screws come from the factory with nylon inserts. If those are worn or you are not replacing them, blue threadlocker can be used to secure them.

In the upper-right corner of the case, the third/fourth-gear shift rail can be seen being inserted into place. Note that it has not yet come out of the shift fork and that the interlock was still in the upright position that it was in when it was initially inserted into the case. (Photo Courtesy David Randal)

The sequence for installing the third/fourth-gear shift fork and its set screw begins by sliding the shift fork on the shift rail as the rail is being inserted into the case. Check that the hole in the shift rail lines up with the set-screw hole in the shift fork before locking down the set screw. (Photo Courtesy David Randal)

Keep the third/fourth-gear shift fork in a position close to the groove in the third/fourth-gear synchronizer. Insert the set screw for the shift fork but do not tighten it at this point. The tapered hole in the shift rail will position the relation to the fork and shift rail. (Photo Courtesy David Randal)

Before tightening the set screw in the third/fourth-gear shift fork, the shift fork needs its final adjustments. Make sure that the shift fork is centered in the groove of the third/fourth-gear synchronizer and that it will be able to move back and forth when activated by the shift rail. (Photo Courtesy David Randal)

the rail have been lined up, install and tighten the screw. The third/fourth-gear synchronizer should already be in the third-gear position (toward the rear of the case), allowing easy access to install the set screw in the third/fourth-gear shift fork.

When installing the shift rails for the forward gears, this is the builder's last opportunity to find and repair any points on them that are causing friction and drag. Resistance on the shift rails creates slower shifting. It only takes a few minutes to polish off any rough or high spots on the shift rail.

If any rough or drag spots are found on the forward-gear shift rails, eliminating them before the final installation will ensure smooth shifting. They can be dealt with easily by using some polishing compound with a high-grit disc on a small drill or grinder.

Sequence 3

Upon completion of installing the third/fourth-gear shift rail and shift fork and installing the set screw in the third/fourth-gear shift fork, that shift fork must be shifted from the third-gear position to neutral.

The third/fourth-gear detent assembly needs to be installed to keep the third/fourth-gear shift rail in neutral. This allows the first/second-gear shift rail to pass over the detent that will be installed above the third/fourth shift rail. Install the third/fourth-gear shift-rail detent into the hole on the outside (driver's side) of the case. The spring follows the detent into the hole on the side of the case. The detent bolt plug follows the spring and also goes into the hole on the side of the case. Before the detent bolt plug's final torquing (25 ft-lbs), coat the threads with Permatex Ultra Grey sealer and torque the plug. The small detent for third and fourth gear goes into the hole in the top of the case that aligns with the outside detent bolt. This hole is also close to the front of the case.

The sequence for first/second-gear detent installation is three parts and contains a variable on the last step. The first step is to insert the correct detent plug into the hole on the top driver's side of the case. (Photo Courtesy David Randal)

After installing the correct first/second-gear detent plug into the detent hole on the top of the case, the second step is to insert the correct first/second-gear detent spring into the same hole. (Photo Courtesy David Randal)

The next step in the third/fourth-gear detent sequence is to insert the spring for the third/fourth-gear detent into the same outside hole in the case. This is the only hole on the outside of the case that is used for a detent. (Photo Courtesy David Randal)

Coat the threads of the third/fourth-gear-detent bolt with sealant and screw it into the case. This is the only bolt used for detents on the outside of the case. (Photo Courtesy David Randal)

Torque the third/fourth-gear-detent bolt to 25 ft-lbs on the outside of the case. This is the only detent bolt that needs to be torqued. It can wait until the other fasteners on the case need to be torqued. (Photo Courtesy David Randal)

This third step depends on the year of the Toploader that is being built. Some Toploaders use a threaded plug, while others use no threaded plug and rely on the top cover to retain the spring and detent plug. (Photo Courtesy David Randal)

If the Toploader that is being built uses a threaded plug, it must be inserted so that it will not interfere with the seating of the cover, which takes place later in the assembly. Screw the plug flush with the face of the case. (Photo Courtesy David Randal)

A threaded detent plug looks like this when it is done. Note that the opening of the hole has been countersunk and the threaded plug is flush or a little below the surface of the case so that it doesn't interfere with the gasket and cover. (Photo Courtesy David Randal)

Sequence 4

The first/second-gear shift fork also needs to be installed before the back main bearing is pressed onto the output shaft.

Position the first/second-gear shift fork in place on the first/second-gear synchronizer. Lubricate the shift-rail bore, rail bosses in the case, and the slot that the shift cam engages on the first/second-gear shift fork. Install the first/second-gear shift rail from the back of the case with the side of the rail with three notches and a set-screw hole facing upward.

Keep the set screw out at this time so that the tapered hole in the shift

The sequence for correctly installing the first/second-gear shift rail begins with positioning the first/second-gear shift-rail detent so that it is ready to drop into its hole in the first/second-gear shift rail. A magnet is used here to position the detent to be dropped into the shift rail. (Photo Courtesy David Randal)

This shows the positioning of the detent plug for dropping into the shift rail. Note the use of a long magnet tool to hold the detent until it's time to go into the shift rail. Another tool is used to push the detent into the shift rail. (Photo Courtesy David Randal)

Using the entering shift rail from the back of the case, attach the first/second-gear shift fork. It may take some wiggling to line up the two pieces correctly. Note the three notches in the shift rail. (Photo Courtesy David Randal)

At this point of the assembly process, the Toploader should look like this. All three shift rails, shift forks, shift-fork set screws, and internal detents are in place. Note the missing pieces of the rear main bearing and input shaft that have yet to be installed.

rail can be seen inside the set-screw hole. This ensures that the set screw will seat in the taper and not just against the outside diameter of the shift rail.

Make sure that the shift rail passes through the first/second-gear shift fork and into the center shift-rail boss in the case until the set-screw hole in the shift rail lines up with the set-screw hole in the shift fork. Note that unlike the third/fourth-gear shift fork, the first/second-gear shift fork needs to be brought in on an angle and then rotated into the correct position on the synchronizer.

In addition, make sure that the cam and shaft's pin engages the slot in the fork of each shift fork. Move the shift fork into position and secure it with its set screw. The first/second-gear shift rail will not protrude from the back of the case while in neutral.

If the Toploader that is being built uses a screw to hold down the detent spring, now is the time to install it. If not, the cover will act as the hold-down when it is installed.

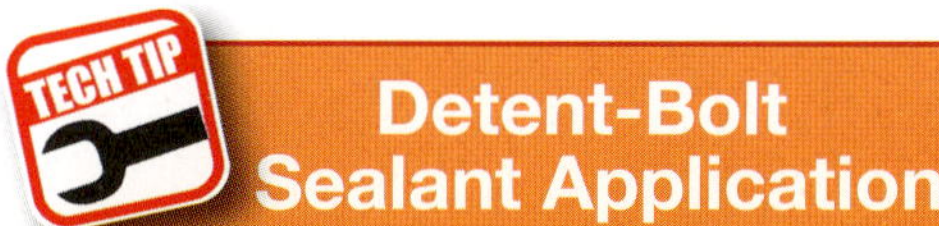

Detent-Bolt Sealant Application

Install the detent bolt on the side of the case and its components without any sealer (at this point) to place pressure on the detent spring. After the transmission has been fully assembled and successfully bench tested, remove the bolt, apply sealant, and torque the bolt into place. ■

Lock down the set screws for the shifter fork. Finally, position the shift fork into the groove in the first/second-gear synchronizer before securing the shift fork's set screw. Check that the shift fork is centered in the groove and not binding anywhere. (Photo Courtesy David Randal)

To begin the sequence for installing the third/fourth-gear detent and its related parts, insert the round-head detent into the third/fourth-gear detent hole on the driver's side of the case. Note that the hole is on the outside of the case. (Photo Courtesy David Randal)

When installing the countershafts, they need to seat into the face of the case. The roll pin will locate into its relief, and the shift rail will be flush in the case. The roll pins lock the shift rails in position.

Two countershafts are shown in their final position in the case. Note that they are flush with the surface of the case. This becomes important when the bellhousing and tailhousing (parts that bolt up flush to the case) are attached.

Sequence 5

The next step in the assembly process is to install the rear main bearing. Installation of the front and rear main bearings can be enhanced with a few simple procedures. These methods were discussed in depth in chapter 4 during disassembly when the builder first encounters those bearings. They were also referred to in the leading paragraphs of this chapter when preassembly operations were discussed. Ideally, the decision to use those procedures was made before assembly began and can now be put into play for this step of assembly.

Make sure that any shift-rail ends are flush in their holes with nothing protruding. The reverse shift rail will protrude from the back of the case with the transmission in neutral. The 1-2 shift rail will not protrude while in neutral.

This photo shows the use of David Kee's temporary (dummy) rear main bearing that is described in the text. It holds the output shaft in its finished location so that you can continue the rest of the internal parts assembly. There is more information about installing the rear main bearings in the text.

After installing the rear main bearing, install the inside and outside rear main-bearing snap rings. Install both to lock down the output shaft in the case. The protruding shift rail that is detailed in the text is shown at the bottom of this photo. (Photo Courtesy David Randal)

The main front bearing is ready to be pressed onto the input shaft. Check this bearing before and after pressing. Look for excessive movement in the ball bearings, seating of the inner and outer rings, and how the bearing operates with and without oil (friction-wise).

For this step, turn the case onto its front face on the workbench with clearance and support around the protruding input shaft if it has already been installed. For installation of the rear bearing, it's easier to work in this vertical position.

When the rear bearing is in its correct position, install the inside and outside snap rings.

Press the bearing onto the input shaft and install the two snap rings (one for the input-shaft bearing and one for the input shaft).

If it has not been done as part of preassembly, coat the input-gear bore with a thin film of oil or petroleum jelly and install the 15 needle bearings. The input shaft uses needle bearings to seat with the tip of the output shaft. The bearings go into the darker and smaller bore in the back end of the input shaft. A light lube will hold the bearings in place for assembly. Note that unlike the needle bearings

Install the input shaft's main bearing by pressing it onto the input shaft (a press is required). In this photo, a special jig is used to complete this task without damaging the engagement gear and its cone. (Photo Courtesy David Randal)

With the input-shaft main bearing correctly pressed into place, install the snap ring. Make sure that the snap ring is centered in the groove all the way around the shaft. The snap ring will be on the shaft's front (engine) side. (Photo Courtesy David Randal)

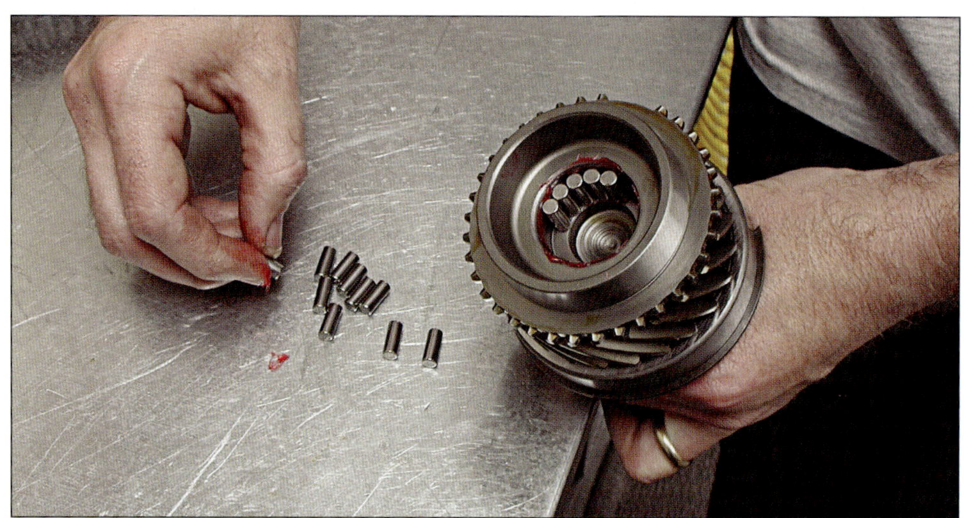

On the transmission side (rear of the input shaft), install the 15 needle bearings. A thin layer of oil or petroleum jelly will hold the needle bearings in place for further assembly. (Photo Courtesy David Randal)

When properly seated in the input shaft, the 15 needle (roller) bearings ride on the front tip of the output shaft. The output and input shafts ride together but are only fully connected when fourth gear is engaged. (Photo Courtesy David Randal)

The input shaft uses 15 needle (roller) bearings to seat with the tip of the output shaft. In this photo, the bearings go into the darker and smaller bore in the back end of the input shaft. A light lube, such as a thin film of oil or petroleum jelly, will hold the bearings in place for assembly. (Photo Courtesy David Randal)

The cone of the input shaft is being lubricated. Continue the practice of coating the components with a lubricant for the initial start-up, as all of the cones are high-friction areas on the output shaft. Take care not to disrupt the seated needle bearings. (Photo Courtesy David Randal)

Fitting the bronze blocking ring to the input shaft is done prior to installing the input shaft into the case and onto the output shaft. The output-shaft pilot needs to ride inside the input shaft on the needle bearings. In addition, make sure that the notches in the blocker ring fully engage the inserts in the synchronizer assembly. (Photo Courtesy David Randal)

With the blocker ring attached, install the input shaft into the large opening at the front of the case. The output shaft should enter the needle bearings in the input shaft. In addition, make sure that the notches in the blocker ring fully engage the inserts in the synchronizer assembly. (Photo Courtesy David Randal)

Lining up the input and output shafts to connect inside the rear of the input shaft may require some manipulation of both shafts at the same time. Using one hand on the input shaft and one hand on the output shaft (as shown) can help you line them up and seat them together. (Photo Courtesy David Randal)

At this point, all of the internals are installed and set in place. The builder's workbench should look something like this. Only the external parts and assemblies are left to install, including the tailhousing, the bearing retainer, and the cover.

Upgrade the Retainer Bolts

A simple but effective upgrade is to replace the factory input-bearing retainer bolts, which can damage the case, with Grade-8 bolts. Coat the Grade-8 bolt threads with Permatex Ultra Grey sealant and torque them to 20 ft-lbs. ■

in the cluster and reverse gears, there is no retainer for the input shaft's needle bearings.

Be careful to not disturb the previously installed needle bearings and lubricate the cone of the input shaft. This cone will seat with the third/fourth-gear synchronizer.

Position the fourth blocker ring on the input shaft gear.

Place the input shaft in the case, making sure that the output-shaft pilot enters the needle bearings inside the input gear, and that inserts into the synchronizer, which engages the notches in the blocker ring.

With the case still in a vertical position, align the cluster-gear bore and thrust washers within the bore in the case. Install the cluster-gear shaft from the rear (or, now, top). It may take some jiggling to get it in and align it with the gear of the input shaft. This will also push the dummy shaft out of the cluster gear. Move the shaft all the way into the bore of the case until neither end of the cluster-gear shaft is sticking out of the case.

Making sure that all connecting surfaces are clean, press the seal into the bearing retainer so that it bottoms out in the bore. If the seal is installed too shallow in the retainer, it will bottom out on the input shaft and

Keep Components from Falling out of Place

A trick that some builders use at this point of the assembly is to insert one of the shorter top-cover bolts into one of the bearing-retainer holes to temporarily lock down the input shaft and keep it from moving forward during further assembly.

This is done because the transmission is usually moved from a horizontal position to a vertical position (and back) during assembly, and loose components can move around and fall out of place.

In the case of the input shaft, when it is not secured, its 15 needle bearings can become dislodged and fall loose into the case. If this happens, the assembly process must be reversed to retrieve those bearings. When the transmission is back in the horizontal position after engaging the input shaft with the cluster gear, the temporary bolt can be removed, and the bearing retainer can be fully installed. ■

damage the seal. A proper fitting tool can help during installation.

Apply a thin coat of oil on the input shaft where the input-shaft seal will contact the shaft. The four holes in the input-shaft retainer are a uniform pattern and can allow for a wrong gasket fit. Align the gasket with the oil return on the retainer. Having test fit the gasket, align the holes so that the oil return is facing down. Lay the gasket in Permatex Ultra Grey sealer that has been applied on the input-shaft bearing retainer.

With the bearing-retainer gasket mounted correctly, make sure that the oil return is facing down and

With the correct-size tool to press the seal into the input-shaft retainer, carefully tap the seal into place. In this photo, a custom-made tool fits the seal correctly and distributes the hammer force evenly to ensure good fitment without damaging the seal. (Photo Courtesy David Randal)

A correctly installed front seal for the input-shaft retainer should look like this if it has been seated properly. Note the lack of hammer marks on the metal edges and the lack of dents in the actual seal element's thin material. Make sure that the corresponding tool fits correctly.

A wise idea by David Kee is to use one of the cover bolts to hold the input bearing in place as the transmission is moved from a horizontal position to a vertical position and vice versa as part of the assembly process. (Photo Courtesy David Kee)

Locking down the input shaft keeps smaller parts, such as needle (roller) bearings, from falling out of position. If that happened, the builder would have to take the transmission apart and restart the assembly process. (Photo Courtesy David Kee)

After lining up the holes in the gasket with the holes in the input-shaft retainer, carefully lay the gasket onto the bed of Permatex Ultra Grey sealer and install it onto the front of the case.

Begin installing the four input-shaft retainer bolts by hand. Then, use a wrench to distribute even pressure with a cross pattern to seat the retainer. Once the bolts are relatively tight, torque them to 20 ft-lbs. (Photo Courtesy David Randal)

install the retainer with its four bolts. Torque them to 20 ft-lbs.

On the part of the output shaft that is extending out of the case, position the speedometer-gear drive ball bearing into its opening in the output shaft. Slide the speedometer gear over the output shaft until it stops in position with its notch over the gear drive ball. The speedometer drive gear attaching method uses either a metal clip or a ball and snap ring. David Kee recommends using the ball and snap ring because the metal clip may come loose, and it allows the gear to move out of its working position. The ball and clip are part of the David Kee Toploader Transmissions rebuild kits.

The tailhousing bushing must be installed correctly to ensure oil flow to the driveshaft yoke. Installing it now, before the tailhousing is bolted to the case, is easier because it can be done upright on a benchtop without

Installing the cluster-gear shaft does two things: 1) It replaces the dummy shaft that was used to keep the needle bearings and thrust washers in place. 2) It engages the cluster gear with the input shaft and forward gears on the output shaft, allowing all of their gear teeth to mesh. Note how the roll pin lines up with the capture hole in the case to keep the cluster-gear shaft from turning. (Photo Courtesy David Randal)

Coating the tailhousing bushing with oil helps with installing it and pre-lubing it for use when the tailshaft seal is installed. It also keeps lubricant in place for the initial running. Note the opening on the tailhousing bushing. (Photo Courtesy David Randal)

Optional Breather

Fitting an optional breather onto the tailhousing can be done at this time because the tailhousing has not yet been bolted to the case.

Drill a "letter R" drill-size (0.339 inch) hole into the seam of the top side of the tailhousing about 1½ inches rearward of the top cover. Next, use a 1/8-inch pipe-thread tap to thread the hole in the tailhousing casting. Remember, as this is cast iron, it will be more brittle than steel, and tapping needs to be "backed off" regularly.

After making sure that none of the threading chips remain inside the tailhousing, install the new breather with Permatex Ultra Grey sealer on the threads. If you use an optional breather, make sure to seal the hole in the stock cover or replace it with a cover without an air vent. ■

Toploader builders have choices for the breather that they want to use. The top arrow points to an aftermarket breather that was drilled, tapped, and installed on the tailhousing. Note how the normal breather on the cover has been closed. The bottom arrow indicates the OEM breather on the top cover. (Photo Courtesy David Randal)

This is the inside of a cover where the factory breather has been sealed. This is a common practice when an optional breather is installed elsewhere. Read the text for options for using a different breather and even relocating it to the tailhousing.

This is an example of an aftermarket breather. It's installed into this tailhousing, close to where the tailhousing bolts to the case. Details for drilling and tapping tailhousings are in the text. The transmission has been painted gloss black.

The tailhousing bushing has an oval-shaped opening that allows lubricant to circulate around the bushing and driveshaft yoke. That opening needs to line up with the recess seen here at the driveshaft end of the tailhousing casting. (Photo Courtesy David Randal)

Using this specialized tool, the tailhousing bushing is gently tapped into its correct position. This tool will push only on the edge and keep the bushing square in its path to locate it into its final position. (Photo Courtesy David Randal)

Note the wide flange that contacts the end of the bushing. The key is for the tool to push only on the bushing and move it uniformly and squarely into its final position (as shown). (Photo Courtesy David Randal)

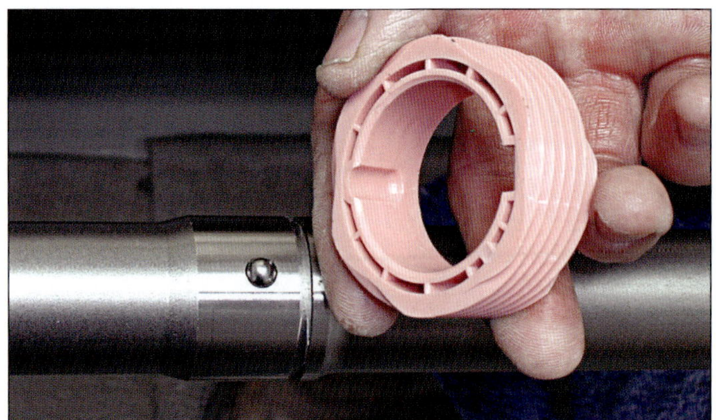

Making sure that the speedometer-gear drive ball is properly installed into the hole in the output shaft, install the speedometer gear in place. Look at the inside of the gear to see the groove for the drive ball so that they can be lined up together. (Photo Courtesy David Randal)

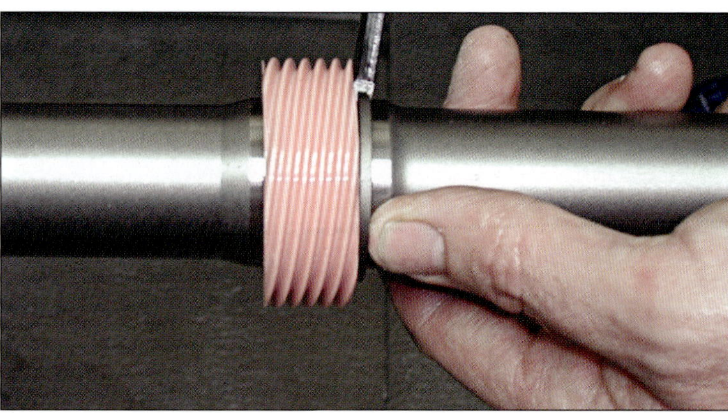

Once the speedometer-gear drive ball is securely in place under the speedometer gear, it needs either a clip or a snap ring to hold the gear in place. Using a snap ring is the preferred method and is shown here being put into place against the speedometer gear. (Photo Courtesy David Randal)

the output shaft getting in the way.

First, coat the bushing with oil and install it with its opening lining up with the small, circular, half-round indentation in the tailhousing. The bushing's oval-shaped opening is for lubricant circulation and needs to line up with the indentation in the tailhousing.

Be careful. The bushing is made from thin material and installing it with too much force can easily deform it. Use a driving tool that best matches the size of the bushing to avoid deforming. It's okay to use a bushing set, a socket, aluminum, or even wood to gently drive the bushing. Specifically, use a number-26-size bushing driver for a 28-spline version and a number-29-size bushing driver for a 31-spline version.

Make sure that all of the countershafts are properly seated into the case. The countershafts have roll pins in the ends where they seat into small pockets in the case. The countershafts must be seated and flush into the case to make sure that the bellhousing and tailshaft can bolt flush and true against the case.

Using a new gasket, secure the tailhousing to the case with the five 5/8-inch-socket-head, 7/16 x 18-inch bolts with standard split-ring lock washers. Use Permatex Ultra Grey sealer on all bolts and gaskets. Put the sealer on the threads of the five tailhousing bolts and torque the bolts to 50 ft-lbs for an iron case. See torque specifications in the appendix for an aluminum case.

One of the most effective methods to check a transmission's shifting action is to find out if it will not

The gasket that goes between the case and bellhousing must be positioned correctly before bolting the tailhousing to the case. The gasket is directional to the bolt pattern and needs to align with the holes in the case. (Photo Courtesy David Randal)

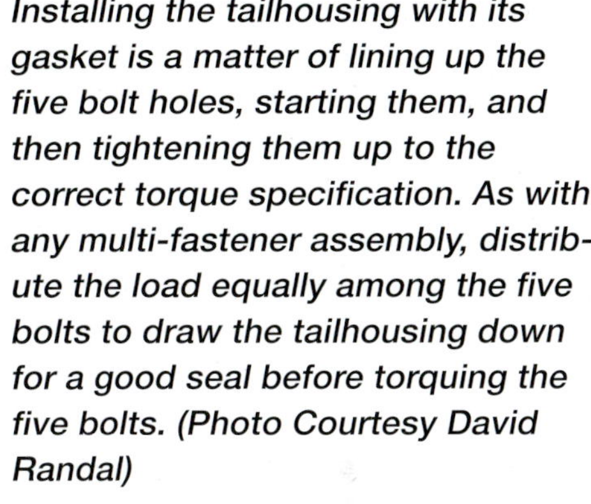
Installing the tailhousing with its gasket is a matter of lining up the five bolt holes, starting them, and then tightening them up to the correct torque specification. As with any multi-fastener assembly, distribute the load equally among the five bolts to draw the tailhousing down for a good seal before torquing the five bolts. (Photo Courtesy David Randal)

Installing the tailhousing onto the case in a vertical position is usually easier than if the case is in a horizontal position. The main reason for this is that gravity will hold the tailhousing in the correct position and help distribute the weight equally for holding the gasket flat and torquing the bolts. (Photo Courtesy David Randal)

go into any other gear when it is in reverse. Doing so (not going into any other gear) shows that all of the detents are installed and working properly. Do this test during the assembly process because if this is an issue, you do not want to discover it after the transmission has been installed in the vehicle.

The bearing retainer and the outside detent bolt must be torqued (if not done previously). Torque the four bearing-retainer bolts to 19 to 25 ft-lbs and torque the detent bolt to 10 to 15 ft-lbs.

Coat the threads with Permatex Ultra Grey sealer and install the filler plug and drain plug into the case if they were removed. Make sure that the magnetic plug is installed in the bottom of the case. Wrench-tighten these two fasteners like an oil-pan bolt. If an optional breather has been used, now is the time to coat the threads and install it if that has not already been done.

When torquing all of the fasteners on the outside of the case, remember to include the bolt for the third/fourth-gear detent. That detent bolt should be torqued to 10 to 15 ft-lbs. It's easiest (regarding leverage) when the transmission is in the horizontal position. (Photo Courtesy David Randal)

Additional fasteners on the outside of the case are the front bearing retainer's four bolts. They should be torqued to 19 to 25 ft-lbs. As with the detent bolt, having the transmission in a horizontal position makes this step easier. (Photo Courtesy David Randal)

If the optional breather that is described in the text is used, install it at this time. Using pipe tape or sealer on the threads reduces the potential for future leaks. (Photo Courtesy David Randal)

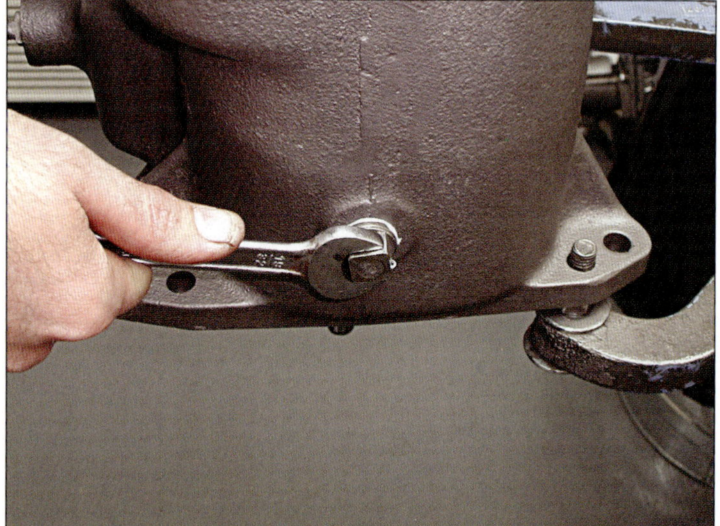

The case's lubricant drain plug (shown here) is on the bottom front of the case and must be tight. Pipe tape or sealer keeps it from leaking—or even coming loose and falling out. (Photo Courtesy David Randal)

Lubricant

David Kee has done extensive research about which oils to use for various Toploader applications. Here are his recommendations:

Oils for Break-In

The transmission should be on a level surface with the opening at the top. Fill the Toploader with any quality 80W-90, GL-4 gear lubricant until the oil level reaches the fill-plug opening. It takes approximately 2 quarts.

I recommend changing the gear lube for the first time between 500 and 1,000 miles. This oil change removes the lubricants (these lubricants have dissolved at this point) that were used to pack the needle bearings. This also removes the floating silicone sealers; threadlockers; break-in metals; and any remaining glass, shot beads, and debris that has settled to the bottom of the case.

In addition, any new parts in the transmission need to seat with others during the break-in period. Because of this, it is not uncommon to see very fine metal shavings on the magnetic drain plug when draining the lubricant for the first time.

Oils for Routine Maintenance

I suggest changing gear lube every 20,000 to 25,000 miles for normal street-driving applications. If you have a higher-than-stock-horsepower engine or you drive your car aggressively, change the gear lube every 10,000 to 15,000 miles. I recommend PennGrade 1 Classic GL-4 Gear Oil SAE 80W-90.

Road-Racing Transmissions

Toploaders used in road-racing applications need their own specific break-in procedure. Put some *easy* (low to mid RPM) laps on the transmission, lightly accelerating and decelerating with each gear. This gives the gears an opportunity to break in and dissolve the lubricants in the needle bearings that were used during assembly. After a few laps like this, drain the transmission and clean the magnetic drain plug. Again, it is not uncommon to see very fine metal shavings on the magnetic drain plug when draining the lubricant for the first time.

Refill with 2 quarts of high-quality, GL-4 gear lubricant. Once this break-in has been completed, the transmission is race-ready. Kee recommends PennGrade 1 Classic GL-4 Gear Oil SAE 80W-90. Check the magnetic drain plug during every subsequent oil change.

David Kee recommends using PennGrade high-performance oil in Toploaders for almost all uses from street to racing. His research in building thousands of Toploaders for almost every use has provided a substantial amount of data regarding which oils work the best and which oils should be avoided. (Photo Courtesy PennGrade)

Synthetic Gear Lubes

Synthetic oil is very popular in the automotive industry today. The way that Toploaders are designed, they need a certain amount of friction for the blocker rings to fully synchronize shifts. Kee has had customers try synthetics, and while some say that they work well, others disagree. However, everyone does agree that standard gear lubricant works. The single largest determining factor regarding whether synthetics will or will not work is the driver.

If you drive your car normally and shift it normally, synthetic is a great choice. If you drive aggressively or want to shift fast, synthetic oil may not work well. If you try synthetic gear lube and it does not work for your driving style, drain the transmission and try standard PennGrade 1 Classic GL-4 Gear Oil SAE 80W-90.

GL-5 Gear Lube

GL-5 gear lubricant should not be used in a 4-speed Toploader due to the extreme pressure additives that are aggressive to the soft metals that are used in some Toploader internal components. ■

Building Options

Some builders opt for a dry-lube finish on the internals for their Toploaders. Dry-lube applications can involve using an aerosol to apply the finish, or the finish can be applied by professionals who bake it onto the components. It's strictly a personal choice or preference. This common treatment is often seen on rear-end gears and engine components.

Pour the lubricant over the entire geartrain while rotating the input shaft. This turns and coats the cluster gear and connecting gears. If you fill the transmission on a bench or outside of its intended vehicle, consider using some sort of plastic plug in the speedometer hole and in the tailhousing until the speedometer cable and driveshaft yoke are installed.

Using an adjustable wrench, turn each shift lever to see how it moves the shift fork and engages and disengages its gears. Remember to return to neutral before testing the next gear. In addition, test the reverse-gear shift lever to ensure that it engages reverse. Note any differences from when it was tested previously without lubricant.

If it has not been already done, install the remaining detent plug above the first/second-gear shift rail in the case hole. Install the long spring to secure the detent plug. If the Toploader that is being rebuilt has a 1964 through early 1968 case, it will need the short detent spring and a set screw to compress the spring. If the case is late 1968 through 1971, the long spring is the correct one. The installed cover will compress the spring in place.

Coat the third/fourth-gear shift-rail plug bore with sealer and install the new expansion plug, making sure that it is seating properly and

This Toploader has received a dry-lubricant treatment. It can be done via an aerosol can or sent out for professional service, where it is baked on. This procedure is common in performance building and is often seen on other driveline components.

When testing the shift levers (as seen here with first and second gear), also test the internal mechanism. Watch and feel for tightness and smoothness as the shift fork moves to engage and disengage its gears. (Photo Courtesy David Randal)

Testing third/fourth gear is shown. Don't forget to test reverse. Note if you are feeling any drag, as that could indicate a problem. This is the last chance to find any glitches that could turn into major obstacles. (Photo Courtesy David Randal)

Liberally apply sealant to the third/fourth-gear shift-rail plug bore and install its expansion plug with a matching-size driver. The plug needs to be seated correctly around its circumference and to lay flat so that it does not interfere with mounting the bellhousing. (Photo Courtesy David Randal)

The third/fourth-gear shift-rail-bore plug should set below the plane of the front of the case if it has been properly installed. The expansion plug needs to be hit in the center to seal around the outside edges. (Photo Courtesy David Randal)

evenly. Install the plug initially with a tool that hits the plug around the circumference. This is an expansion plug, so push the center of the plug to fully expand it for its final fitment. Builders working on numerous Toploaders use an old shift rail for its complementary fitment. The plug needs to sit flush as to not interfere with the fitment of the bellhousing.

The two extra holes in the top-cover gasket that are not for the perimeter top-cover holes are for the OEM vent hole in the top cover. They should not line up with any of the cover-bolt holes.

It sounds simple, but don't forget to make one last check to make sure that the lube is at the correct level before fastening the cover for the final time. Check one last time for the positioning of the cover gasket even though it can only fit one way.

Install the cover, making sure that

When the next step is installing the cover, a finished Toploader should look like this inside. This is a great reference photo to make sure that the components are in proper order and the gear teeth are facing in the correct direction. (Photo Courtesy David Randal)

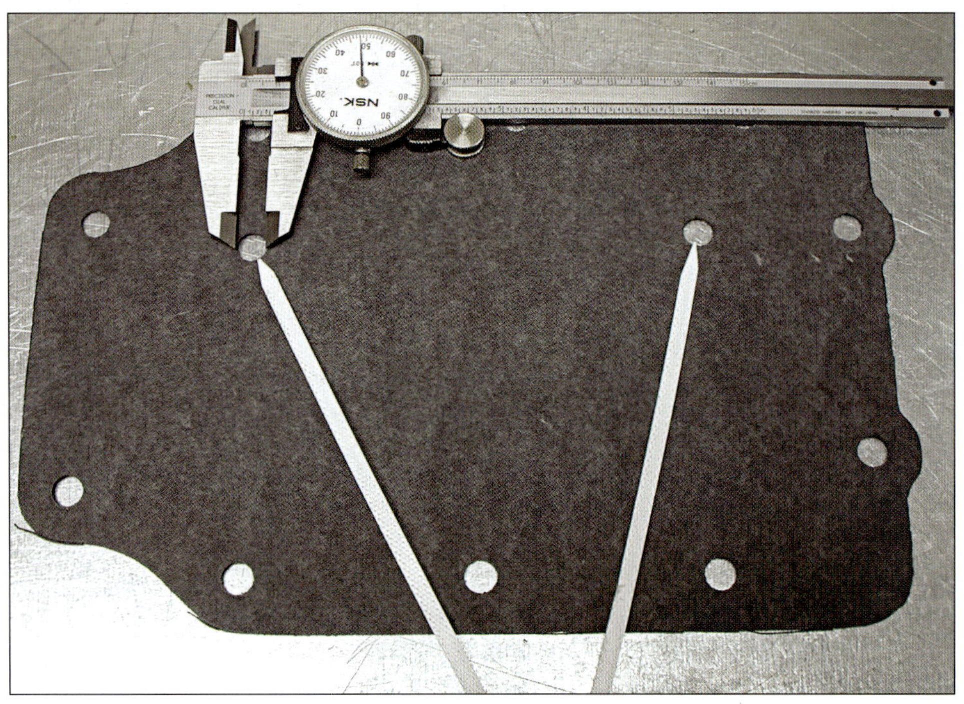

Most replacement gaskets have two extra holes in them that are used as baffles to allow air to escape without oil/lube escaping. The extra holes are pointed out in this photo, and they are located away from the cover-bolt hole pattern around the outer edge of the gasket. (Photo Courtesy David Randal)

It's important to use the correct fasteners on the cover. The best ones have serrated washers for additional grip. Remember that there are 10 total bolts, but 2 are longer than the others (as shown). (Photo Courtesy David Randal)

Do not forget to apply a sealant to the 10 cover bolts. Driveline components receive the bulk of driving vibrations, and the constant upshifting and downshifting of a transmission causes vibrations as well. If the cover comes loose, the road grime that would enter the transmission would cause abrasive damage. (Photo Courtesy David Randal)

A Toploader cover uses 10 bolts, and 2 of them are longer than the other 8. Make sure that all of the hex heads of the bolts are not damaged and that the bolts have proper working threads. The last thing that any builder wants is to strip the threads in the case. (Photo Courtesy David Randal)

the two longer bolts are in their correct locations. The two 1-inch-long bolts go into the machined dowel holes on the driver-side front corner and passenger-side rear corner. Test the fitment first to make sure. Apply Permatex Ultra Grey sealer to the 10 cover bolts' threads and install them. Tighten the bolts to 15 ft-lbs.

Now, install the Toploader into the car and break it in properly.

The two longer cover bolts go into the machined dowel holes on the driver-side front corner and passenger-side rear corner. To prevent warping of the cover, torque the bolts evenly across the cover at 15 ft-lbs. (Photo Courtesy David Randal)

If a Toploader builder wants a total restoration, it should look similar to this one. This build uses a color of paint to simulate the factory cast iron, and the paint will prevent it from rusting like a factory cast-iron piece. (Photo Courtesy David Kee)

This restored Toploader will be installed into a completely restored Mustang. Desirable features include a readable code tag, cast-iron-simulated paint to avoid rust, and an easily accessible fill plug. This one even has readable casting numbers.

Ford High-Performance Toploaders

The Ford high-performance Toploaders are available in two types: 1) the ultra-rare original transmissions that were made by Ford's performance department in the 1960s and 1970s for use in its own factory race cars, and 2) the aftermarket high-performance Toploaders that were produced after the factory Toploaders finished their run. The aftermarket Toploaders are covered in chapter 8.

Ford's high-performance Toploaders were factory-built, 4-speed transmissions that were used on oval tracks, drag strips, and road courses. In the overall scheme of special, high-performance Toploaders built by Ford, surprisingly few were produced. Road racers received the bulk of these rare and special Toploaders, and many of them were used by competitors in the Sports Car Club of America's (SCCA) Trans-Am series. In the Trans-Am series, Ford's popular Mustangs faced off against Chevrolet Camaros, Plymouth Barracudas, American Motors Corporation (AMC) Javelins, etc.

In road racing, downshifting is just as important as upshifting. That's where having the best gear ratios specially dialed in for each track pays dividends for race teams. It's also why more gearsets with additional ratios became available to those factory Ford race teams.

In racing, especially factory-backed racing against other manufacturers, any advantage was exploited in the quest to win. In the big picture, changing a few gearsets and the corresponding cluster gear in a transmission that was hand built for racing was a quick, simple, and cost-effective way to gain an advantage. If a particular track had one or two turns that would contribute to that advantage with a little more or less gear, it was worth building new and special gear ratios and cluster gears.

From a manufacturing viewpoint, having sets of gears and cluster gears made was much less expensive than designing and creating something more complex, such as a new intake manifold or set of heads. In racing, gearing is always used to get the optimal RPM at various locations on the track.

As with oval-track racing, road-racing teams wanted the most power just before the location on the track where they would begin deceleration. In addition, teams wanted that power to kick in when the driver resumes acceleration, which is almost always coming out of a turn. Those old racing basics were behind what would come to be known as Ford's "White Stripe" Toploaders.

White Stripe Toploaders

White Stripe Toploader racing transmissions were used in Ford factory race cars—primarily for Mustangs in SCCA Trans-Am road racing. White Stripe Toploaders were aptly named due to a white stripe that was painted by the factory Ford Toploader builders across the top, flat part of the passenger's side of the case.

This stripe was painted over the casting numbers on iron cases to quickly indicate being a limited edition. The stripe gave no indication of the gears that were inside. Instead, that was left to the five-letter tag-code system that was already in use on production models. However, instead of the usual metal tags that were riveted to the case, the extremely rare White Stripe versions had HEH prefixes and suffixes that were hand-stamped onto the cases.

The gear ratios chosen were custom tailored to the car and/or track. The ratios were selected to gain every possible advantage against the competition. Ford had successful performances, winning two SCCA Trans-Am Series championships during the four golden years that the Detroit builders were actively involved.

By 1971, the factories had mostly left the series because the popularity of the pony cars waned at dealerships. With rising insurance costs and the first oil embargo in 1973, the handwriting was on the wall for muscle cars in general. Still, the short-but-sweet White Stripe Toploader history is cool, and seeing the unusual gear choices that were created is interesting.

The HEH code group for White Stripe Toploaders had 12 gear-choice combinations that are shown in the table below, which was compiled by David Kee.

Those noticing that the last three models (HEH-HG, HEH-HJ, and HEH-HK) had a different gear ratio for first gear and reverse are probably wondering how that is possible. Due to the tooth-count changes that were necessary to achieve such a high first gear, the reverse idler gear that is in constant mesh with the cluster gear had to be changed.

Since reverse is driven from a second idler gear to achieve reverse rotation of the output shaft when the tooth counts are calculated in all but these gearsets, the first gear ratio ended up being the same as reverse. Making just one gear-tooth change on one gear in play will make a difference. When the diameter of gears is changed, there is a limit to the number of teeth that can be added or subtracted. Adding or subtracting teeth on one gear usually affects the tooth count on any gear that it is in constant mesh with.

When building these three special transmissions, the builders had to make sure to use that correct first gear and include the special reverse idler gear with the now-different reverse gear ratio. As with any other gear-ratio change, a new and matching cluster gear had to be created and installed.

Code	Ratio	First	Second	Third	Fourth	Reverse
HEH-HH	Wide	2.74	2.00	1.40	1.1	2.74
HEH-HF	Wide	2.54	1.85	1.30	1.1	2.54
HEH-HL	Wide	2.54	1.69	1.24	1.1	2.54
HEH-HM	Wide	2.54	1.55	1.14	1.1	2.54
HEH-HA	Close	2.32	1.69	1.29	1.1	2.32
HEH-HB	Close	2.32	1.54	1.29	1.1	2.32
HEH-HC	Close	2.32	1.54	1.19	1.1	2.32
HEH-HE	Close	2.22	1.43	1.19	1.1	2.22
HEH-HD	Close	2.13	1.56	1.19	1.1	2.13
HEH-HG	Close	2.02	1.54	1.14	1.1	1.96
HEH-HJ	Close	1.84	1.42	1.14	1.1	1.72
HEH-HK	Close	1.76	1.36	1.14	1.1	1.65

Another note about the last three White Stripe Toploaders that are listed in the table is that they all share the same third-gear ratio of 1.14. While that third-gear ratio was also used in the HEH-HM White Stripe model (a wide-ratio unit), the last three units with the different reverse gear ratios are close-ratio units and also have that 1.14 third gear. In addition, all three of those different units have a lower first-gear ratio than all of the other units.

One can't help but notice how the ratios kept inching lower numerically with these three transmissions and how that related to the second-gear ratio as well. Was this to enable the driver to drop to a lower gear when entering a tight turn and then have plenty of power for exiting?

It was extremely unusual for road racers to downshift to first gear with these normal, street-geared transmissions. First gear was almost always for leaving the pits. Second gear was about as low as a driver would usually go for tight hairpin turns. Some tracks may have had turns where the exit was short before entering another quick turn, and a launch was needed but not for a long time.

With the ratio that was used, racers had the peak of their power range while coming out of tight turns. Who knows what kinds of tricks the lower gear ratios would allow drivers to pull with first gear having what would ordinarily be the same ratio as second gear? Maybe they used first gear more than they said they were using it. Maybe *that* was the idea for these special road-racing Toploaders.

Factory part numbers for these gears were etched onto the gears by hand due to the limited quantity. They contained the usual "X" designation for "experimental."

Factory Aluminum Cases

While White Stripe Toploaders are very rare, the lightweight, aluminum-case versions were even rarer. According to David Kee, only about 10 aluminum cases were created for road-racing use.

The mid-to-late 1960s was the time when all OEMs increased using aluminum for production castings, and that trend quickly included aluminum heads and other more complex components and assemblies, such as gear cases.

In 1969 and 1970, at the height of Ford's factory participation in SCCA Trans-Am Series racing, the casting numbers were a giveaway as to the material used. The castings were marked "XAA 12512 ALCOA 2" with the usual "X" prefix for "experimental." The "ALCOA" part of the designation left no doubt as to the type of material used for the case.

The units also had an HEH-HG code hand-stamped on the upper corner of the passenger's side instead of the usual metal tag that was riveted to the case. One likely reason for their limited production may have been that Ford no longer would be involved with SCCA Trans-Am racing shortly thereafter.

Lee Holman, of Holman-Moody, said many believe that some Toploader cases cast from magnesium were created for Ford factory drag racers. However, this has not been confirmed. Holman also explained that the T-44 transaxles that were used in the Mark 4 and 7 big-block Ford-powered GT40 road racers contained some Toploader parts. Since the GT40s had transaxles, the overall configuration was different, so not all of the Toploader's parts fit their needs.

Now, about 60 years later, it's hard to believe that these were the only custom or high-performance Toploaders that Ford made in-house for all of those years and all of those factory racers. As active as Ford was in all types of racing at that time, it would have likely had performance Toploaders for each of its other types of cars in drag racing and oval-track racing as well. Instead, those genres of racing used their own ideas and aftermarket shops to improve on the Toploader.

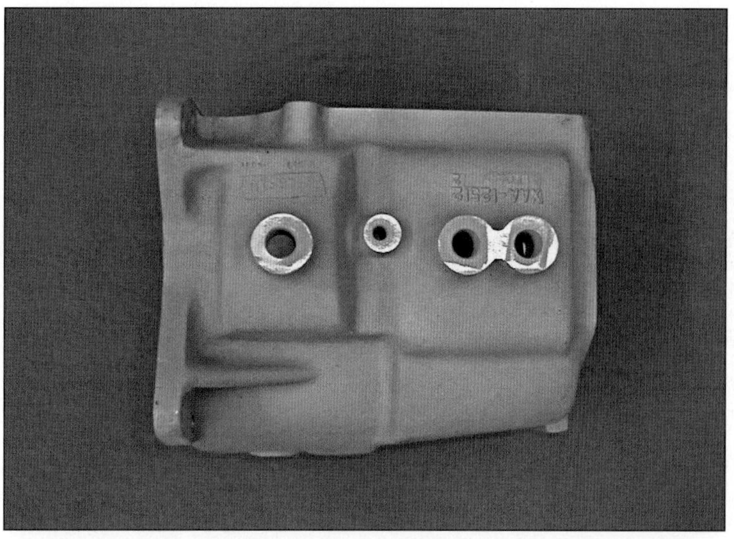

One of the original Alcoa aluminum Toploader 4-speed cases that was made for factory race teams shows its smooth-grained aluminum casting finish. This makes it look like it's been surface prepped or painted, as opposed to the usual rough-grained cast-iron finish. (Photo Courtesy David Kee)

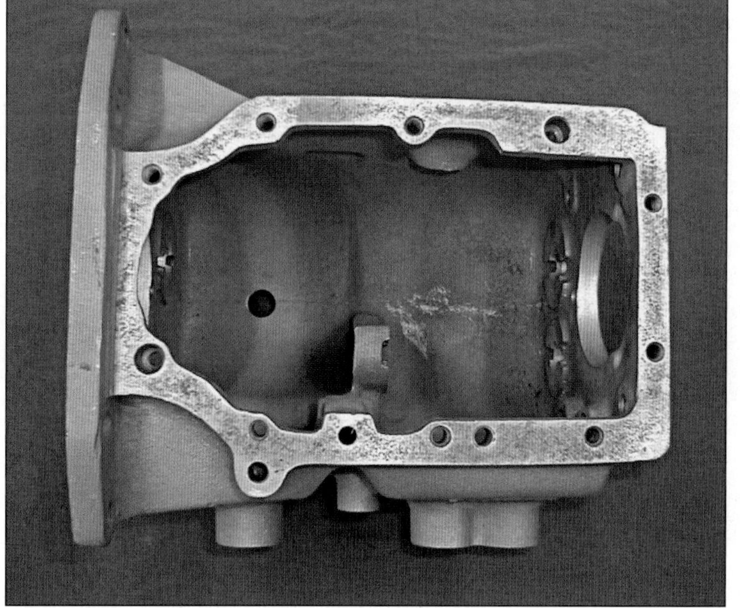

This is the Alcoa aluminum Toploader 4-speed case that was made for factory race teams. The lighter-appearing areas have been machined just like the cast-iron pieces were. This contrast also shows the details of the two bolt holes for the cover that use the longer cover bolts. (Photo Courtesy David Kee)

Transitional High-Performance Toploaders

As the engines and transmissions evolved on the track, the evolution and legend of the Toploader advanced as well. In 1964, Ford made sure that there were Toploaders in the new 1964 Super Stock 427 Ford Fairlane 500 Thunderbolts and, later, in the 1965 B/FX 289 Comet Cyclones. At about the same time, they were used in what many believe were the original Ford Funny Cars.

Drag-racing Mustangs in the A/FX class with 427 single-overhead-cam (SOHC) engines were evolving on drag strips across the country as part of the popular Funny Car madness. These one-off cars used Toploaders until technology caught up and such cars were switched to beefed-up automatic transmissions.

Ford racers in other forms of drag racing were still using Toploaders, and the more enterprising race teams were learning how to make them stronger and more reliable as horsepower levels steadily increased. They all had their secrets and continued to do so, as those improvements were perfected and more performance and reliability were realized.

NASCAR was already a stable for Ford teams heading up a strong factory presence in the mid-to-late 1960s. Racers there were using Toploaders and eventually evolved them into purpose-built 4-speeds, using many of the Toploader's design features. Toploaders worked their way up to the top in NASCAR, and as part of NASCAR's evolution, their use was not limited to Ford racers. NASCAR was already known for taking components and assemblies from one manufacturer and making them standard for the industry—even using them in competing brands.

One example is a Ford 9-inch rear end being installed on a Chevy truck's rear suspension. Regardless of what engine and body was on the car, that setup featured the approved parts, and all of the brands used them. This was done in NASCAR for many years before switching to an independent rear suspension and transaxle in 2022.

In addition, Toploaders were used behind some of the famous Chrysler Hemis in Dodges and Plymouths in NASCAR. From suspension designs to transmissions, teams used parts that would last the grueling 500-plus miles of a race, regardless of the original designing manufacturer. What began as a factory part or assembly was redesigned and built better and stronger by teams and aftermarket companies that specialized in such parts. Racing teams did this on their own in search of any possible advantage.

In the top attractions of motorsports (drag racing, road racing, and oval-track racing), the performance Toploader was here to stay. The many great ideas that Toploaders had developed for racers and enthusiasts over the years were not just going to fade away. They were too good and in too much demand, as they stood atop the OEM units of the time. Instead, in its new life in the aftermarket, the Toploader morphed into even better, more effective versions of itself. In addition, the Toploader's popularity resulted in brand-new 4-speed transmissions being created.

CHAPTER 8

AFTERMARKET HIGH-PERFORMANCE TOPLOADERS

All of the 1960s' 4-speed transmissions from Detroit's Big Three manufacturers, including the Ford Toploader, had outlived their service lives by the late 1970s. Detroit did some gear shifting of its own, either flatlining the evolution or ceasing the building of regular 4-speeds altogether. That opened the door for another type of performance Toploader: the aftermarket high-performance Toploader.

These new Toploader versions, some strictly for racing and some built with varying degrees of street manners, were created by aftermarket companies. They effectively contributed to the continued evolution of the Toploader. These aftermarket high-performance manual-transmission builders cultivated the best of the Toploader's design elements, added fresh new ideas and improvements, and made newer and better transmissions for the racing and performance industries.

Similar to the restoration market, automotive aftermarket businesses first carried the Toploader's history forward by making replacement parts. However, these companies didn't stop at replacement parts. They improved on the original Ford design, tweaking a part here and an assembly there.

Using many of the same basic metal and machining techniques that were used in the engines with those rapidly increasing horsepower numbers, the weak points of a Toploader were studied, dissected, and rebuilt to be stronger, faster, and more effective. However, this process was not 100-percent smooth.

Folks who were seriously analyzing the new parts noted that when the pieces stopped coming from Ford, the well-defined specifications that generally come with OEM parts also stopped in some applications of aftermarket versions. Hard specifications, such as material quality, the heat treating processes, and especially the way that the all-important gears were cut, were now often being done differently. These decisions were business-oriented.

Big companies, such as Ford, considered these factors to avoid parts breaking and excessive warranty work. So, it factored in extra reliability within the specifications and generally made better pieces while making considerably more of them.

So, the aftermarket, not always having the resources to put that kind of research, machining, or money into a part or an assembly, often came up short. One example is cutting gears.

Gear Cutting

The OEM manufacturers use dedicated gear-cutting machinery, and the many technical aspects of a normally complicated gear is perfect for each piece. However, aftermarket gear vendors may not have or be able to spend the money to match the factory methods and specifications. Aftermarket companies may use a shaper or shaver to make their smaller run of gears, and the radius and valleys between the teeth could be slightly different.

The gears may work on a street version, but when they are installed into a high-end performance application, those small differences eventually become an issue. This affects performance and service life. So, additional time was required for the aftermarket to improve the Toploader.

Evolved Toploaders

Aftermarket racing transmission builders took up the cause and made mostly new racing transmissions that were "carry-ons" or later evolutions of the Toploader. These pieces eventually morphed into complete purpose-built transmissions with straight-cut gears that still looked and operated distinctively like Toploaders—only much better. These new pieces quickly evolved into all-new units that retained their Toploader lineage characteristics.

I included this look into Toploader evolution for two reasons. The first reason is to see how incredibly advanced they have become. The other reason is to educate Toploader fans regarding which features are available for improving or even replacing their Toploaders, as some of the companies that are featured offer such services.

Researching Toploaders quickly reveals that several companies have built performance and racing transmissions with roots coming from the Ford Toploader. These builders range from those building just Toploaders or clones to some with completely unique ideas. Either way, they represent the current "carry-on" status of how Toploaders have evolved since Ford stopped producing them. A few of these builders are described here.

Andrews Products

Andrews Products (andrewsproducts.com) is one of several companies that helped Toploaders evolve. Its products are still used today in NASCAR, the Automobile Racing Club of America (ARCA), and Trans-Am racing. Being primarily a gear-oriented company, it invested heavily in CNC equipment that could cut gears the best way. One of its first improvements dates back to 2002, when it designed and began making its own Toploader gears.

The NASCAR Cup cars that Andrews Products serviced made 900 rear-wheel hp. The original factory Toploaders were only designed for 200 to 300 hp. In 2000, Andrews Products discovered how flexing the output shaft affected downshifting when it would push the output shaft lower in the case.

In road racing, this affected the geometry and alignment of the shaft, its gears, and how they all engaged and disengaged. Andrews Products built a 30-percent offset into the main shaft, so that under the stress of downshifting, the face of the gears is straight and in the proper geometry alignment to mesh effectively. The company also "crowned" the lead onto the gear teeth to help the gears mesh more quickly. Instead of two flat-gear-face surfaces engaging, the gears first edge load and then fully seat with the mating gears. Andrews Products added dogs, pockets, and sliders to eliminate factory-style synchronizers to make gear changes even faster, smoother, and more "locked in."

Today, Andrews Products still services current race teams, where teams can rebuild their Andrews Products transmissions as often as after every race. Teams also have the option to own or lease the transmissions from Andrews Products and utilize a regular maintenance schedule.

The Andrews model A431 maintains some Toploader design in that it played into a big evolution change. This change also has an interesting but evolutionary take on the shifter and its rods/linkage. When NASCAR's Car of Tomorrow was being designed for its debut in 2007, one of the safety goals was to move the driver a little farther away from the door. The main obstacle was the transmission's shifter tower and linkage. The answer was to move the shifter and linkage to the top of the transmission, locating it along the tailhousing's centerline instead of beside the tailhousing, closer to the driver. That was easy for the shifter, as basically all it needed was some new locating brackets.

The shifter rods were another story, and that took advantage of the most familiar trait of Toploaders: the top-mounted cover. Now, instead of having the shifter rods connect to the cams and levers on the side of the case, they were rerouted to the top cover. Inside the A431, the synchronizers (by now advanced to dogs and sliders) were moved to the top of the box, where the newly located shifter rods connected and actuated the gear changes. The result was being able to move the driver's seat over a reported 4 inches for added safety. Once again, having access to the case via the top cover (now with newly located shifter-linkage ports) keeps the transmission easy to work on and strong in design.

The Andrews Products A431 unit has more than just a different and improved shifter location. Inside the transmission (which is compatible with all drivers and track types), state-of-the-art CNC gear cutting, grinding, and inspection equipment are used to make reliable gears that have won races. This package transfers high horsepower and torque to the rear axle and is available in 24 gear ratios.

Cobra Automotive

The sleeper of all the Toploader carry-onward performance transmissions is from Cobra Automotive (cobraautomotive.com). In addition to offering service on OEM Ford Toploaders, Cobra Automotive sells what it calls the "ultimate in stealth racing transmissions." Used in racing classes that require stock and original parts, this exclusive unit looks every bit like a Toploader because the case and tailhousing are just that. However, inside the OEM case are the performance advantages of a Jerico transmission. Cobra Automotive begins with stock Toploader iron cases and tailhousings, custom machines them, and then installs Jerico internals.

After seven to eight hours of machining the case and tailshaft to make extra clearance for the Jerico internal components (including a physically larger gearset), Cobra Automotive drills an extra detent hole and increases the cluster-gear shaft size. The shifter-shaft surfaces also need to be machined as well as the front bearing shaft diameter size, which receives a bigger front case bearing. Likewise, the tailshaft housing is enlarged for a bigger and stronger bearing. While Cobra Automotive is working on the tailshaft housing, it is modified by increasing the size of the drainage passage and oil return. A new vent is also added to the tailshaft housing.

With all of the machining done, a new set of Jerico internal components can be used for the full benefit of their superior design. Cobra Automotive created a gearbox that has all of the Jerico features with the exception of the stronger aluminum case. This includes all of the Jerico gear ratios. Cobra Automotive advises that the Toploader's iron case can crack at the upper left-hand mounting ear, so the installation and mating-surface condition are important to avoid mounting ear failure.

"The purpose for this transmission [is] primarily to use a dog ring, straight-cut-gear-type transmission in an environment where the obvious use of a purpose-built racing transmission is not legal," according to Cobra Automotive. "It serves this purpose well, but when engaging the transmission into first gear in a pit or paddock situation, it is obvious that the gearbox is not a synchro-type unit because of the audible clunk that it makes going into gear."

With this hybrid transmission and its internal components that are undetectable from outside of the case, users get the best of both worlds. Jerry Hemmingson, the creator of the Jerico, worked with Cobra Automotive in the 1990s to develop this unique piece. Cobra Automotive builds this transmission to order, which allows for tuning to the specific vehicle and its use. In addition, the company created its own shifters for this unique application.

Cobra Automotive also offers performance work for OEM Toploaders.

"Our Toploaders are built with the knowledge that we have regarding which components will best survive in a competition environment—the best replacement internal components, bearings, seals, synchronizers, and blocker rings, etc.," according to Cobra Automotive. "We also try to match the gearset, main shaft, and other critical large rotating components for compatibility, keeping in mind that some aftermarket parts have alloy differences that may create a failure. We check certain critical clearances and properly vent the gearbox for competition use. We have built many Toploader transmissions for use on the West Coast, Europe, and other racing venues that require period-correct transmissions."

For regular Toploader inspections, Cobra Automotive checks clearances between the main shaft and the contact inside-diameter surfaces of the gearset. If needed, it hones those dimensions to the proper tolerances for better oiling and to eliminate the possibility of any gears welding themselves to the output shaft.

These race-prepped Toploaders offer close-ratio gears that have been honed for increased oiling. Bearings in these units have been upgraded to premium grade. In addition, a Hurst Pro-Billet Shifter is available. These units come in both 28- and 31-spline output shafts as well as 1$\frac{1}{16}$ and 1$\frac{3}{8}$-inch, 10-spline input shafts for small- and big-block Fords, respectively.

In addition, Cobra Automotive sells Jerico transmissions, offering your choice of gear ratios.

ETG

Earnhardt Technologies Group (ETG) creates state-of-the-art manual transmissions for short-track and oval-track racing. Coming from Dale Earnhardt Incorporated, the same team that the seven-time NASCAR champion created and owned, ETG (earnhardttechnologiesgroup.com) has been marketing a large line of components for short-track cars for more than a dozen years. For the short-track market, it provides suspension parts, driveline components, tools, setup equipment, and a large number of miscellaneous parts used for dirt and pavement race cars.

As with the other companies that are listed in this book, ETG transmission products have strong Toploader roots. Its 2-, 3-, and 4-speed

Showing its Toploader roots with the cover on top, this is an Earnhardt Technologies Group (ETG) transmission. The shifter assembly has been moved to the top of the transmission, it uses a single shaft for shifting, and it still retains the basic 4-speed look. (Photo Courtesy Earnhardt Technologies Group)

transmissions are not for NASCAR Cup cars and trucks or for the street. These pieces are custom built and used in short-track racing across the country. They are a great example of what the Toploader has evolved into for hard-core oval-track racing.

ETG decided to make its transmissions with its own parts when the company ran into problems getting parts from outside vendors. It designed its own cases and tailhousings, first making 3-D prototypes before sending them out to be cast. The finalized cases and tailhousings are made of magnesium, and a premium is paid for that material because it is lighter than aluminum.

The company uses vendors to create ETG-designed gears and shafts. Most internal components get coatings and micropolishing to decrease friction and heat. In addition, ETG believes that less is best and keeps it uncomplicated when it comes to inside components.

As for transmission designs, ETG utilizes the best and current ideas of today's racing industry. That level of technology revolves around dogs and sliders instead of synchronizers. ETG also designed and manufactured its own shift systems that are based on the T5 for its one-shaft simplicity. Quality driver feel is the goal, and the company pays attention to the throw and gate movement of shifting, which is similar in feel to the units that were used in Corvettes.

ETG doesn't sacrifice static weight for gear strength and knows that racers are very weight conscious. The ETG philosophy is in educating the racer/buyer to not only ask about how much ETG transmissions weigh but also to learn how they contribute to the car's center of gravity and components mounted below the chassis centerline. According to ETG, you should look at how the transmission contributes to the car's handling by helping with controlling the additional weight required by most racing associations. Usually, when a car has to add weight to make rule minimums, it is located in the frame rails. However, the transmission, which is typically in the center of the car and partially below those frame rails, is a better place for weight.

G-Force Transmissions

G-Force Transmissions (gforcetransmissions.com) offers a large number of high-performance transmissions for a variety of uses. Its GSR model closely resembles the Ford Toploader the most. It's a 4-speed that uses a single rail with an internally shifted design. The center shaft is supported by two bearings, keeping shafts and gears in alignment while under typically heavy racing loads. G-Force uses an integrated midplate for even more internal support. In addition, there's an optional internal oil pump that is unique to the GSR model.

The internal shifting feature is directly incorporated into the top plate of the transmission. This allows the shifter to be located in the center of the transmission, offering the driver a safer position more toward the middle of the vehicle. The internal shifting mechanism used in the GSR has been found to help the driver make positive shifts that can be very quick without having the transmission "hang" between gears.

G-Force's GSR has a traditional 32-spline output shaft and can be built with virtually any input shaft for almost any application. The case and tailhousing are cast of high-quality magnesium to reduce weight, and they feature internal and external cast reinforcement. Aluminum is an option for the case material.

Cases and tailhousings are coated for surface protection, making cleaning easier. Gear ratios are interchangeable. GSRs come with G-Force's proprietary-designed long shifter. The GSR can be adapted to almost any bellhousing, clutch, and throwout bearing and spline combination.

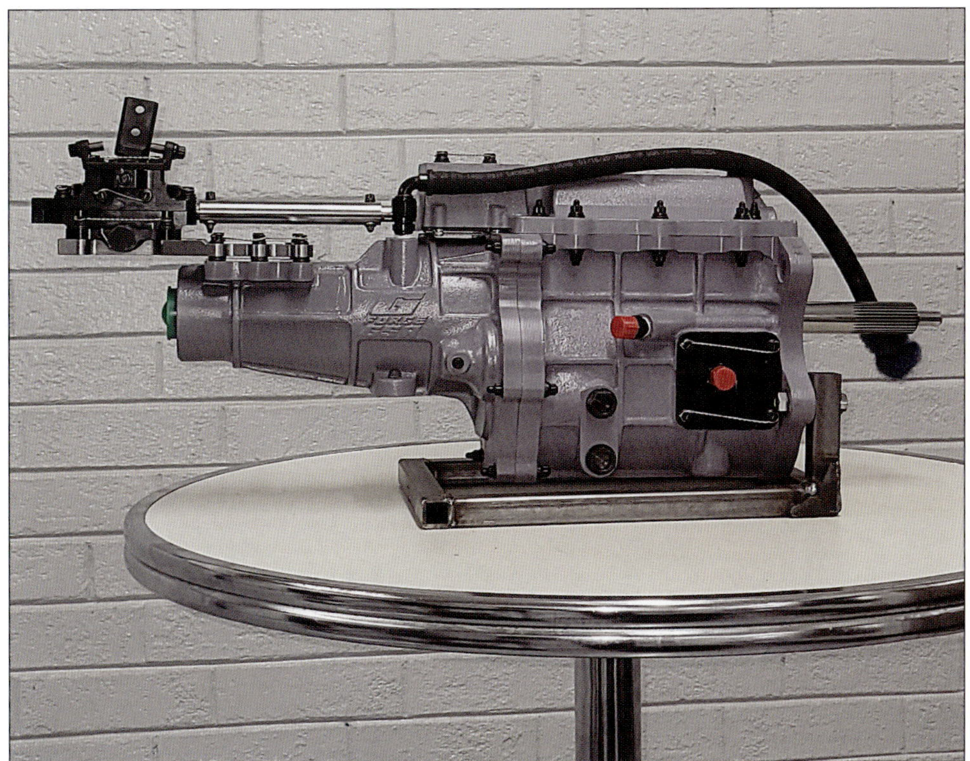

The GSR model from G-Force Transmissions is a 4-speed with strong Toploader roots. It features the evolutionary relocation of the shifter to the center of the unit and offers the usual Toploader opening location. Note the provisions for cooling, the different mounting locations, and the overall stoutness of the casting pieces. (Photo Courtesy G-Force Transmissions)

Liberty's Gears

Liberty's Gears (libertysgears.com) builds Toploaders in original and modified formats and has been doing so since the 1960s. It took on Toploaders when they first came out and quickly learned ways to increase their performance. Today, Liberty's Gears can improve your Toploader with two operations: pro shifting and face plating.

Liberty's Gears removes the stock synchronizers and enlarges the engagement window on the gears for faster, higher-RPM shifts. In fact, the company stated that there is an unlimited RPM range, virtually no chance of jumping out of gear, and the worry of missed shifts is eliminated. Pro shifting uses shift lugs to engage on the inside of the slider.

One of the areas common with slider-shifting technology is the pro rings wearing from normal use. They create burrs that require dressing, deburring, and possible replacement. Liberty's face plating promises less wear on the components used for engagement, making it cost effective. The lugs are on the face of the slider, keeping them from creating burrs and additional maintenance during use. The design of the face-plate shift lugs yields additional contact areas, making them much more durable. It also increases longevity.

Note that the Liberty's Gears pro shifting and face plating will not make for clutchless shifting. Shifting with lugs and sliders creates a large shock load, and not using the clutch would cause severe damage to the transmission.

Liberty's Gears offers cryogenic processing of parts to increase dimensional and core stability and to add to fracture and wear resistance. The company also offers thermal stabilization, shot peening, and surface enhancement. Surface enhancement is unique, as it finishes the surface by blending peaks and valleys to reduce surface friction.

Getting a Toploader updated for today's usage is rather easy, considering the many options that are available for performance 4-speeds. It just comes down to selecting which evolved version of the Toploader fits your 4-speed needs.

THE PROGRESSION FROM TOPLOADERS TO JERICOS

Loyal Ford racers have no doubt pondered how the Toploader would have evolved for modern-day performance and racing. It's no secret that the evolution is the Jerico transmission. With Ford not investing into any Toploader upgrading efforts, the task fell to the performance aftermarket and the Jerico.

The first step in the evolution of Ford's first 4-speed came from the unlikely sport of snowmobiling. In 1972, Jerry Hemmingson was racing as a professional snowmobile racer and was involved in a serious racing accident. The injuries broke Hemmingson's shoulder and shattered his right elbow, resulting in nerve damage that left him with less than 100-percent use of his right hand.

"I learned to work with the other hand," Hemmingson said.

The damage resulted in the end of his professional snowmobiling career. While recovering from the accident, he turned the bulk of his energy to the other type of racing he was doing at the time. He was able to continue drag racing, but shifting with his damaged right arm was now painful. He used a bungy cord to assist in the difficult second-to-third-gear shift, but he needed a better solution.

Hemmingson moved to the A/Gas class with his Pinto-bodied racer. While he broke the NHRA record, he also broke a number of Toploaders. When rebuilding them, he had more than just parts replacement in mind. He wanted to make them stronger, lighter, and faster.

This was about the time Ford that dropped the Toploader from production, so Hemmingson took a look at the future of not only Ford's 4-speed but also racing 4-speeds in general. The changes that he was making were made at an opportune time for the racing industry. Developing his own Toploader cases, tailhousings, and gearsets, he was noticed by the racers that he was beating on a regular basis. In fact, his success during a five-year run was enough to have some competitors challenge his unique transmission modifications with sanctioning bodies.

"We were always legal," Hemmingson said. "They figured that I shouldn't be able to shift it that quick, especially being handicapped."

The result was a line of racers who wanted to buy Hemmingson's spare Toploader parts. Soon, his trailer became a shop, and his racing operation became Jerico. Hemmingson's Jerico transmissions, which were used in drag racing, NASCAR, and road racing, featured the simple but highly effective and logical progression of the Toploader.

The evolution from a bone-stock Toploader to what became a Jerico transmission involved Hemmingson looking at literally each and every component and improving upon it. Some of these mental exercises began as far back as during his healing time from the snowmobile accident. Many of the original aspects of the Toploader design were kept for their simplicity and effectiveness. Hemmingson began his journey by replacing broken parts with those that he redesigned and manufactured.

In a *Tooling & Production* article, where Hemmingson discussed Jerico transmissions in detail, he revealed that all of the work was done in-house except for the castings and heat treating. His changes and evolution were so all-consuming that I broke them down to specific areas to better understand just how much was improved in creating this new industry standard.

The first big difference was the mechanics of building a transmission. Racing parts are never designed for long production runs like the components the OEMs design and build. Jericos were designed to be quick, effective racing pieces. In fact, most of the improvements listed here are in direct contrast to what an OEM would do for running production parts and assemblies. Factories use larger tolerances as well as more liberal (faster) production methods. However, this was the Jerico journey that the Toploader took to carry on after the mid-1970s.

Hemmingson began with better gears and casting pieces. By the time that his units became a household name in racing, he had redesigned and improved virtually every part. Along the way, he incorporated new ideas, and that total sum of parts make up a Jerico. I begin with his philosophies of machining and move onward to the specific changes that were made to the components.

Today's Jerico performance transmission looks like this. Note the large number of billet pieces. Even the case and tailhousing are billet. Such pieces are stronger and easier/faster to make than many cast pieces. The cover still uses 10 bolts to hold it down—just like an original Toploader. (Photo Courtesy Jerico Performance Products)

Production Methodology

Keeping close tolerances requires attention to detail. Usually, the aim in machining is for plus or minus 0.005 inch. Jerico targeted not having any plus or minus—instead, landing on the exact specification.

"We don't tolerance our parts. We go straight for the specific number—the exact tolerance," Hemmingson said. "In this business, plus or minus just isn't close enough. While there's no such thing as perfect in an imperfect world, that's exactly what we strive for."

It was a simple idea, as gears with a closer tolerance help in their efficiency of smooth, precise shifts and operation. Along with the many other ideas that were incorporated, performance levels climbed.

Using state-of-the-art machines in its shop, Jerico devised ways to take advantage of its superior machining ability and quality to achieve positive results. One example is the production of the complex cluster gear. Batch production runs of cluster gears would be machined for the finish of all external surfaces, the machine would be reset, and then all of the internal sizes and finishes would be machined. This process reduced setup, production, and run times. In addition, batch production kept stock on the shelves.

Output Shaft

The output shaft (where strength and precision are critical) and its various diameters presented a machining challenge. Keeping in mind that there is more than one length of the main shaft for various models, this adds up to even more setup/programming and machining time.

However, Jerico worked around this by using a machine that can do the rough grinds, dress its own tooling, and then put the finish grinds on the shafts—all without the part leaving the machine until the process is complete. Working time was reduced by 75 percent, critical dimensions were in line, and there was a reduction in scrap pieces.

Materials

When redesigning stock parts, the materials can be upgraded as well. Using bearing-quality and high-nickel steels, such as the 9310 alloy, Jerico made billet steel gearsets and shafts that would be stronger, take more punishment, and last longer.

Shift Forks

While Ford made its shifting forks simple and effective, Jerico took that component, redesigned it, and upgraded it to a billet steel piece for strength and function. There is plenty of beefy reinforcement in all of the stress points, as these are the pieces that engage the equally beefy slider and dog assemblies.

Jerico also reduced the size of the shift forks compared to the original design, taking advantage of the inherent strength that came with the new billet design. This was one of many moves that greatly reduced overall mass.

Gears

Hemmingson said that all types of racers prefer a Jerico transmissions because they are easy to shift. That begins with a unique gear design. Jerico transmissions don't use the standard Ford helical-gear-tooth design and material. Instead, Jerico opted for vacuum arc remelting (VAR) straight-cut gears.

Straight-cut gears channel the kinetic energy into turning gears in a straight direction on their shafts instead of pushing it away from that axis on an angle. It also distributes the torque load more evenly onto the contact areas of the teeth. Other benefits to using VAR straight-cut gears include reduced rotating mass and less drag. In addition, straight-cut gears require less surface face on the gear to be effective, so a gear face that has less width can be used, which also reduces rotating mass.

About the only downside to straight-cut gears is that they create more noise, which is usually low on a racer's priority list.

Output Shaft

Other steps that Jerico has taken toward maximum performance include increasing the diameter of the output shaft and converting it to be a roller style with the use of Torrington bearings. The result is that the larger and stronger output shaft now runs more true and with less drag.

In addition, the rollerized output shaft runs at reduced temperatures, which delivers more horsepower to the rear wheels because less power is lost to friction during rotation. To complete the package, even the reverse gearset shaft was rollerized for the same reason.

Top Cover

Even the iconic cover for the Jerico's case shows today's racing flavor. Instead of the usual steel Toploader stamping, it is now cast aluminum like the case and tailshaft housing. In addition, the Jerico cover is finned to dissipate heat.

Weight

A stock Toploader weighs about 118 pounds, and Jerico's standard transmission, with its A206 aluminum cases and tailhousings, weighs 44 to 46 pounds less (72 to 74 pounds).

It turned out to be a well-executed design/production exercise, as inside those aluminum cases, the gears, bearings, and shafts have been made sturdier and often bigger in size, yet the total transmission weight is still significantly lighter. In addition, magnesium is offered as a choice for the case material.

Standard Features

Jerico's standard features include polishing operations on shafts and related items for friction and weight reduction. All gears and shafts are cryogenically treated. Cryogenic treatments expose pieces to temperatures below -190°C (-310°F), where much of the stress is removed and wear resistance is increased. This process works on steel and alloys such as aluminum. Coatings for the cast-aluminum case and tailhousing are available.

Gear Selection

Jerico (already working with racers in various motorsports disciplines, including asphalt, dirt track, drag, and road racing) offers more than 200 different gear ratios with overdrives up to 0.85:1.

Heat Treating

Another aspect that Jerico has improved is how it heat treats its gears for different types of racing. Road-racing gears are harder in their heat treatment and are even designed with fuel mileage in mind, while drag-racing transmission gears are softer, as they take more of an instant load during launch and shifting and need to flex more than road-racing gears.

From Synchronizers to Sliders and Dog Rings

The improvements that have previously been discussed are impressive and make for a stronger and better 4-speed transmission. However, most of the Jerico's improvements deal with what was done to the already-advanced Ford synchronizers and the mechanism for changing gears.

To help Hemmingson on those tough second-to-third-gear shifts that his damaged right hand and arm had to make, he designed a slider and dog-ring combination. It eliminated the gear-change issues and made for faster shifts—much faster.

Fast and crisp shifts are sought in all forms of racing, but standard synchronizers can jam between those faster shifts. To thwart this issue, Jericos use sliders that engage more directly with dogs on the gears. The dogs have ring teeth that are wider and spaced farther apart than stock transmissions. The sliders have lugs that lock with the dogs more quickly, which results in faster shifts that don't spend any time passing through neutral like stock transmissions do.

In stock Toploaders, cones make the actual contact between the gear and the synchronizer that are rotating at different speeds. The cones are coated in oil, and their function is to transition between two different speeds. Stock synchronizers work by using the cone for the transition, and then the gears on the synchronizer's blocker gears engage when the two components finally share similar speeds enough to mesh. In essence, the cones must match up the difference in the two different speeds, and they do so by slipping into each other.

In a dog-ring gear box, there are no synchromesh components to acclimate the speed differences between gears. The dogs engage as they move into positions in the opposing surface of the drive gear. Dogs can have angles cut into them to act as ramps to make for quicker engagement. Some styles of dogs have small ramps or angles, while other angles can transcend the entire dog surface. They are somewhat triangle shaped, and that helps them mesh and lock the two gears together quickly. In addition, the dogs are webbed, giving them more strength for those hard and fast connections.

"The transmission engages on the face of the gear tooth, which is more like a motorcycle transmission than a conventional synchronized transmission," Hemmingson said. "This makes for a very fast, smooth shift."

The dogs are cast into the gear face, as part of the gear. Dog gears are much stronger than synchronizer gears due to the thickness of the dog gears. The room for that new thickness comes from the space gained by not having to use synchronizers. This helps to keep component alignment operating at maximum efficiency.

One more Jerico trick is to slightly modify the gears for a car's specific type of racing. Road-racing gears have square-cut lugs on the sliders that are designed for better down shifting, while drag-racing gears (that do not downshift) have what is called an "angled ramp" on the coast side of the slider.

A common myth is that dogs and straight-cut gears are mutually exclusive. This is not true. It is true that they both work better in unison, but a transmission does not need to have both features.

To further simplify this unique system, you are either in gear or out of gear with dogs and sliders, and the recommended method of shifting is fast and direct. Taking a few seconds between the gears can hurt this system, undoing its sole function. In other words, it's not to be driven as one does with a street transmission. This one is for racing only, and it works because there are much fewer and much larger dog teeth than are on a normal synchronizer. That means that the gears are either fully engaged or fully disengaged.

One of many advantages of this system (and one that helped Jerico become a household racing name) is that when the driver backs off the gas during upshifting, using the clutch is not always needed. Downshifting without a clutch is also possible if the driver matches the engine revs to the speed of the gears. The most common way to do that is with the heel-and-toe method on the pedals. In this time-honored procedure, braking can also be included into the downshift.

Oval-Track Racing and Drag Racing

Drag racers weren't the only ones using Jerico transmissions. NASCAR turned to Jerico in the 1970s for reliable transmissions. Hemmingson built transmissions based on the way they would be used, so a drag-racing version was substantially different than an oval-track version.

The same held true for road racing, where shifting in both directions was more of a necessity. Still, the overall theme of the upgrade was the use of new and better parts.

"Until we began building our transmissions for NASCAR in the 1970s, the teams pretty much used standard, synchronized 3- and 4-speed transmissions supplied by the auto companies," Hemmingson said. "What we learned very early is that if you get it stock, off-the-shelf, it won't last in racing. If you can buy it, you'll break it. If it works on the street, it's not ready for the track. You have to make racing transmissions, design the shafts and the gears, and make the shafts and the gears for the high stresses and torque of racing. Just about every type of racing requires a different type of transmission."

With that in mind, Jerico offers transmissions from 2-speeds to 5-speeds.

It didn't take long for Jerico's ideas to spread in the performance world. Today, many of the features are found on other high-performance and racing transmissions. Sadly, the performance world lost the genius of Jerry Hemmingson in 2021. Luckily for racers and performance fans, his Jerico name and what he did with Toploaders is alive and well.

Parts and Torque Specifications

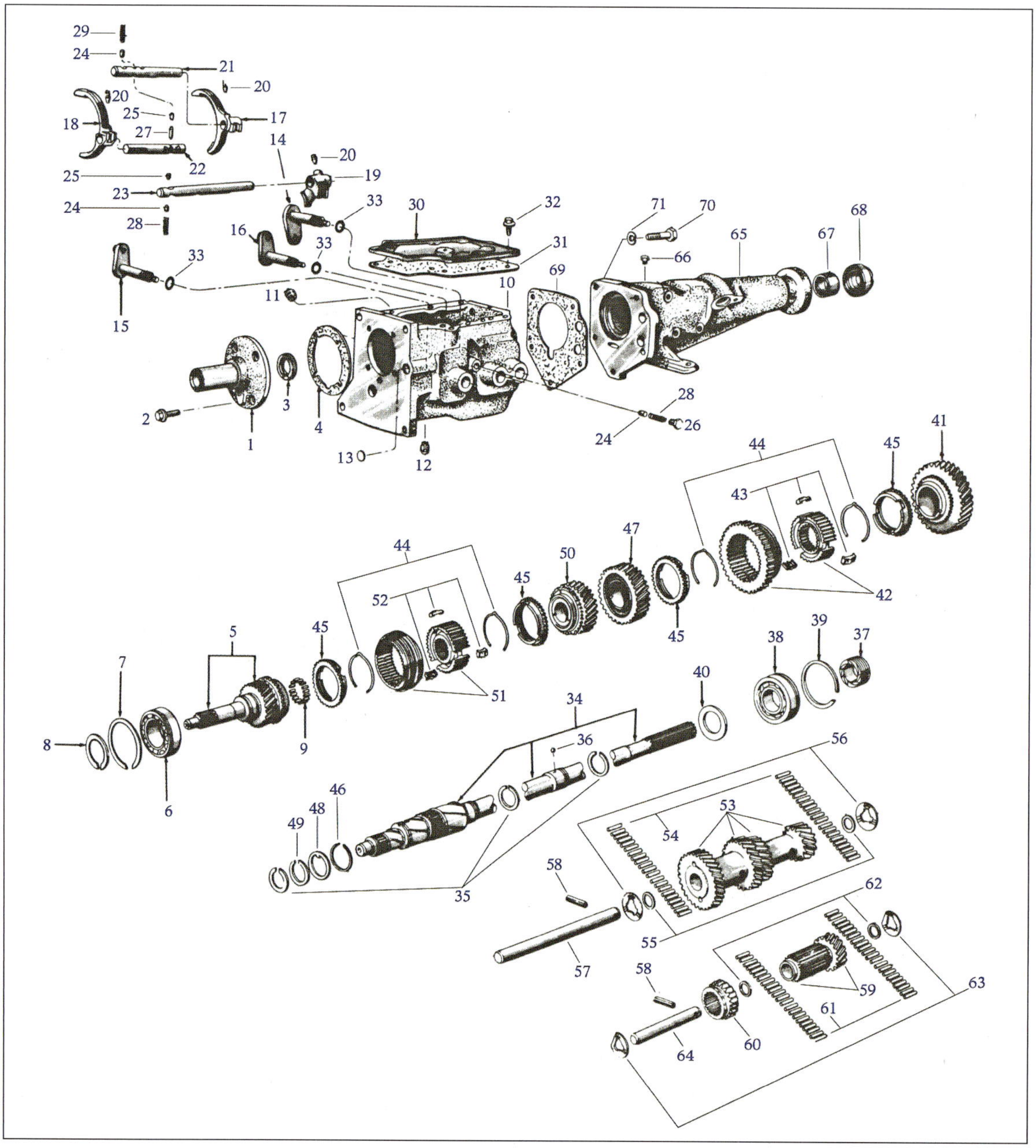

David Kee compiled the following list for the parts that comprise a typical factory Toploader. (Image Courtesy David Kee)

Number on Illustration	Part	Quantity Needed
1	Bearing retainer	1
2	Bolt	4
3	Front seal	1
4	Gasket	1
5	Input shaft	1
6	Front bearing	1
7	Snap ring (for bearing)	1
8	Snap ring (for input shaft)	1
9	Needle bearings	15
10	Main case	1
11	Fill plug	1
12	Magnetic drain plug	1
13	Case plug	1
14	1-2 cam and shaft	1
15	3-4 cam and shaft	1
16	Reverse cam and shaft	1
17	1-2 shift fork	1
18	3-4 shift fork	1
19	Reverse shift fork	1
20	Set screw	3
21	1-2 shift rail	1
22	3-4 shift rail	1
23	Reverse shift rail	1
24	Detent (round)	3
25	Detent (hatchet head)	2
26	Bolt (side detent)	1
27	Interlock pin	1
28	Detent spring (short)	2
29	Detent spring (long)	1
30	Top cover	1
31	Top cover gasket	1
32	Bolt (top cover)	10
33	O-ring	3
34	Output shaft	1
35	Snap ring	3
36	Steel ball	1
37	Speedometer drive gear	1
38	Rear bearing	1
39	Snap ring (rear bearing)	1
40	Thrust washer (first gear)	1

Number on Illustration	Part	Quantity Needed
41	First gear	1
42	1-2 synchro assembly	1
43	1-2 synchro keys	3
44	C-spring	4
45	Bronze blocker ring	4
46	Snap ring	1
47	Second gear	1
48	Thrust washer	1
49	Snap ring	1
50	Third gear	1
51	3-4 synchro assembly	1
52	3-4 synchro keys	3
53	Cluster gear	1
54	Needle bearing	42
55	Needle bearing retainers	2
56	Thrust washer	2
57	Cluster-gear shaft	1
58	Roll pin	2
59	Rear reverse idler gear	1
60	Reverse idler gear (slider)	1
61	Needle bearing	44
62	Needle bearing retainer	2
63	Thrust washer	2
64	Reverse gear counter shaft	1
65	Tailhousing	1
66	Air vent	1
67	Bushing	1
68	Seal	1
69	Gasket	1
70	Tailhousing bolt	5
71	Lock washer	5

Installing parts with the correct torque specifications is essential for operation and parts longevity. Always double-check the measurement units—is it in ft-lbs or in-lbs? Make sure that the torque wrench or tool has been calibrated for accuracy. If fasteners are not held in place correctly, they may move into contact positions and cause damage.

A total Toploader rebuild is not always needed. Sometimes, it's only necessary to replace a part or two to get back on the road or complete an update. Other times, a complete rebuild kit may be necessary.

Either way, rebuilding and repairing a Toploader is most effectively done when you know which parts actually need to be replaced. I included a breakdown of the rebuild kits that are offered by David Kee Toploader Transmissions, which is a leading supplier of Toploader parts.

Torque Specifications	
Location	**Torque (ft-lbs)**
Cover to case bolt	15
Filler plug to case	10–20
Flywheel (7/16-inch bolts)	60–65
Drain plug to case	20–30
Input-shaft bearing retainer to case bolt	20
Outer-gear shift levers to cam nut	20
Pressure plate (5/16-inch bolts)	30–35
Shift fork to shift rail screw	10–18
Shifter plate to tailhousing bolt	20
Tailhousing to case bolt	50 (iron case); 40 (aluminum case)
Third/fourth-gear shift-rail detent bolt	25

David Kee Toploader Transmissions offers several rebuild kits based on how in-depth a rebuilder wants (or needs) to get. The Master rebuild kit comes with the standard-duty SKF bearings that are used to rebuild any 4-speed Toploader. These kits are available in any shaft/spline size configuration, and configuration specs will be needed when ordering. Here are the four Toploader shaft/spline combinations:

- $1\frac{1}{16}$-inch input, 28-spline output
- $1\frac{1}{16}$-inch input, 31-spline output
- $1\frac{3}{8}$-inch input, 28-spline output
- $1\frac{3}{8}$-inch input, 31-spline output

The David Kee Toploader Transmissions Standard-Duty SKF kit contains the following:

- Detent springs
- All needle bearings
- Snap rings
- Thrust washers
- Spacers
- Speedometer ball
- Dowel pins
- Case plug
- Shift lever O-rings
- Front and rear seal
- Gasket set
- C-springs
- New magnetic drain plug
- Counter shaft
- Four bronze, original equipment blocker rings
- Front and rear main bearings
- Synchronizer keys
- Tailshaft bushing
- Instructions

The David Kee Toploader Transmissions Small Rebuild Kit (part number DK296-SPK) fits your choice of the following combinations:

- $1\frac{1}{16}$-inch input, 28-spline output
- $1\frac{1}{16}$-inch input, 31-spline output
- $1\frac{3}{8}$-inch input, 28-spline output
- $1\frac{3}{8}$-inch input, 31-spline output

Reputable Toploader suppliers usually have a well-stocked inventory because they know which parts will be needed for varying degrees of rebuilds. That's why knowing what parts will be needed when ordering works well for the builder. (Photo Courtesy David Randal)

This shows the evolution of a reproduced Toploader part. The part on the right is a reproduction synchronizer component that is no longer available. The part on the left is the same synchronizer part, but it was redesigned (and improved) by David Kee to be similar to the original Ford part. Minimizing the mass contributes to the longevity of the transmission. (Photo Courtesy David Randal)

The David Kee Toploader Transmissions Small Rebuild kit contains the following:

- All needle bearings
- Snap rings
- Thrust washers
- Spacers
- Speedometer ball
- Dowel pins
- Case plug
- Shift lever O-rings
- Front and rear seals
- Gasket set
- Synchronizer C-springs

For quick refreshing of a Toploader, the David Kee Toploader Transmissions Small Parts Kit contains the following:

- All needle bearings
- Snap rings
- Thrust washers
- Spacers
- Speedometer ball
- Dowel pins
- Detent springs

For road-racing rebuilds, David Kee Toploader Transmissions offers a Road Race Kit, again for the following shaft/spline size configurations:

- 1 1/16-inch input, 28-spline output
- 1 1/16-inch input, 31-spline output
- 1 3/8-inch input, 28-spline output
- 1 3/8-inch input, 31-spline output

The David Kee Toploader Transmissions Master Road Race Rebuild Kit comes with max-duty SKF bearings that are used to rebuild all 4-speed Toploaders and contains the following:

- Detent springs
- All needle bearings
- Snap rings
- Thrust washers
- Spacers
- Speedometer ball
- Dowel pins
- Case plug
- Shift-lever O-rings
- Front and rear seals
- Gasket set
- C-springs
- New magnetic drain plug
- Counter shaft
- Four bronze original equipment blocker rings
- Front and rear main bearings
- Synchronizer keys
- Tailshaft bushing
- Air vent
- Three shift-rail set screws
- Instructions

The David Kee Toploader Transmissions Seal and Gasket Kit contains the following:

- All gaskets
- Front and rear seals
- Three shift lever O-rings
- Rear bushing
- Case plug

As with other kits, orders must specify shaft/spline sizes from the following combinations:

- 1 1/16-inch input, 28-spline output
- 1 1/16-inch input, 31-spline output
- 1 3/8-inch input, 28-spline output
- 1 3/8-inch input, 31-spline output

In addition, David Kee Toploader Transmissions offers a complete line of parts for Toploaders from its own aluminum cases and tailshafts to input/output shafts, gears, and virtually every part needed for building a Toploader.

"As the world's largest manufacturer of high-quality 4-speed Toploader parts, we now manufacture every single part of the 24-inch-length, 4-speed Toploader," Kee said.

In addition, David Kee Toploader Transmissions sells ancillary products, including clutches, linkages, flywheels, and shifters. Visit DavidKeeToploaders.com to learn more.